Books and Awards
Patton Howell

Embodied Mind

Fully Alive
Golden Texas Pen Award

Nobel Prize Conversations, Editor

A Journal for Human Science, Editor

War's End
Bronze Medal International Publishers Association

Beyond Literacy, Editor
Benjamin Franklin Award, best literary nonfiction in the United States

PEN Texas Essay Award

Napa Valley, Editor

Self Through Art and Science, Editor with James Hall

Locked Into Life, with James Hall

PEN Texas Lifetime Achievement Award

THE TERRORIST MIND
IN ISLAM AND IRAQ

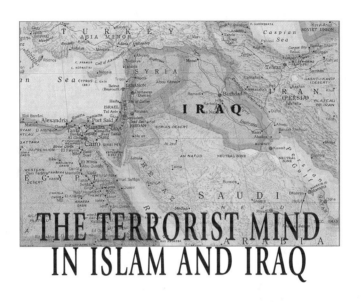

THE TERRORIST MIND
IN ISLAM AND IRAQ

A Guide for Healing Hatred

by

Patton Howell

Library of Congress Cataloging-in-Publication Data

Howell, Patton, 1921-
  The terrorist mind in Islam and Iraq : a psychological study / Patton Howell.
    p. cm.
  Includes index.
  1.Terrorism--Psychological aspects. 2. Terrorists--Psychology. 3. Hate. 4. Social perception. 5. Islam--20th century. 6. Islamic countries--Civilization. 7. Civilization, Modern. 8. I Title.

HV6431.H694 2003
303.6'25'0882971--dc 21

                                          2003041511

Cover design by Fred Huffman
Photography by Gwyneth Howell

Saybrook Publishing Company
3518 Armstrong Parkway, Dallas, Texas 75205

Printed in the United States of America,

Dedication

This is for my wife, Joan.

Table of Contents

CONTENTS

HATRED

MODERNITY

A NEW WORLD

CONTENTS

Acknowledgments

I want to acknowledge my gratitude to my editors Marcelline Watson and Cathy Lombardi, without whom the book would not have been possible; to my old valued friends Jean and Dr. William Tedford; to my dear friends Mary Ann and Donald McComber for many helpful suggestions; to my children Elizabeth Howell, and Lisa and Lawrence Bramlett; to Dolores and Elroy Lehmann for offering invaluable "on the Arab street" suggestions, and to Dr. Rick Lange, Don Montgomery, and Lim Meng Hong for opening many doors to East Asia.

I am grateful to my dear friend, Frederick Turner, for permission to quote from his book, *Seven Blind Men and an Elephant, A Study in the Interpretation of Religion*, and from his poem, *Flight 93*.

I am also grateful to Sultan Succar for graciously sharing his wisdom.

Finally, I acknowlege Rhonda Winchell Sharp for her help in bringing this book to the public.

Further, I wish to thank Saybrook Press for permission to quote from previous books of mine, *War's End* and *Beyond Literacy*; The Nobel Prize Committee, for the quote from Naguib Mahfouz; and the Harvard Club of Malaysia for quotes from a speech by Seri Dr. Mahathir bin Mohammed.

Lastly, I want to acknowledge the public figures in the book who bear their own names, and private characters who have assumed names.

Flight 93

by Frederick Turner

If I had ten million dollars
And a white house by the sea,
I would trade them both gladly
To have been on flight 93.

If I'd won the golden prizes
And the great world honored me,
It would count for nothing if I could
Have flown with flight 93.

Pennsylvania dreamed below
In summer's last green reverie
When they rushed the cockpit, broke the door
And brought down flight 93.

REALITY

I

WHAT IS TRUE

CHAPTER 1

The Terrorist Mind

Terrorism is an ages old disease. However, until recently, terrorists did not have the weapons to wreak mass destruction. If they became more than a nuisance, the state always had the means to wipe them out. So a terrorist act served most effectively as a device for drawing attention to an ideology or a cause.

But the whole world turned upside down when the World Trade Towers in New York City were destroyed. A means of mass destruction had been activated. Terrorism had, or would soon have, the capability to destroy the United States—it had already monstrously embraced the suicidal will to destroy. Suddenly, the terrorist mind was no longer merely an irritant. It had emerged as the most horrifying reality of our world and its future.

Each of us remembers what he or she was doing on September 11, 2001. My wife Joan and I were in London working on an international program to award young people prizes for writing. But everything changed when the World Trade Center was attacked. People in London were saying that democracy had been attacked, humans' last hopes had been attacked. They looked at Joan and me with such pity and compassion. Flags were lowered to half mast, and Joan and I cried. Then the American Embassy was framed by flowers. People came individually and placed them along the street. And again we cried. We could feel that we personally were part of a global family, a family of human beings that finds inclusion through love and hope for the future. But there is also a small world family of *terrorists* that thrives on exclusion through hate.

This book is a call to each person in the Islamic *and* modern cultures to actively join the war on terrorism. We must recognize that the terrorist mind exists everywhere. At the moment most terrorists are Moslems and their targets of choice are Americans, but we must also recognize that Moslem terrorists attack their own Islamic states as well—as Iraq's Suddam Hussein did against Iran in the 1980s and later against Kuwait, prompting the Gulf War. So we are not being attacked by Islam; we are really allies of Islam in this war against terror.

As we approached the one-year anniversary of the terrorist attack on the World Trade Center, eerily, I found myself being asked to consult about a United States' war against Iraq. Looking back on Iraq's bellicose history, we can only conclude that now is the time for us to stand behind our country—whatever our country's decision is. As Americans facing the stark reality of Moslem terrorists, we must first understand Islam and then understand modernity. Only then will we be able to understand the special place Iraq holds in the ongoing war on terrorism.

We must accept that our war will last many years. And this book is designed as a tool to help nonterrorists through those years. This is a new kind of war waged on two fronts—military and mental. And it belongs to each of us, whatever our nation or religion. Each of our individual lives is threatened by death no more nor less than are soldiers' lives.

And although you and I may hold different kinds of ideas and faiths, we must communicate in terms of inclusion and trust to win this war.

Terrorists have no uniforms and live among us. They move among nations. Terrorists hate and will kill whenever they can. Everything except hate and death is excluded from their lives of darkness which oppose individual lives of light.

We are at war with this destructive, murderous hatred. This war is excruciatingly real. It is about the concrete reality of people like you and me being killed. For you cannot negotiate with people who hate you. They only want to kill you. There is nothing you can give to a terrorist to save your life—nothing—not money nor food nor new cars. He will take all such things and use them to kill. The only way to stop the killing is to change the way he thinks.

Each individual terrorist is so full of hatred that he is incapable of perceiving reality. He does not see the difference between right and wrong, good and evil. Still, there is no reason for us to hate him. We can't ask terrorists to be better if we are not. So we must look first at ourselves. There is hope for reversing the indoctrination of hatred, but despising terrorists is not the way to approach their thinking.

Right now the United States is center stage. Individuals in the rest of the world are going to be judging the quality and character of citizens of the United States. Our government changes every four years, but the character of individuals remains the same. Will we be seen as free of hate for our terrorist adversaries? Will we be seen as inclusive of all kinds of people? Will we be seen as trustworthy and concerned with the well-being of all nations? These are the realities of everyday people.

I am a forensic psychophysiologist (forensic—law, psycho—mind, physiology—body). I specialize in how we humans relate to how we think. As a consultant to humanitarian programs in Moslem countries and in this country, I have had an opportunity to learn how some individuals become terrorists.

To recognize the terrorist mind, we need to understand the psychology of terrorism. And since we are all infected with psychological problems of hatred, humiliation, impotence, and self-pity, the first step toward curbing terroristic tendencies is to concentrate on our own minds so that we can help ourselves and others turn away from terrorism. To fight this war we must all, Islamics and modern people, become better people—kind, inclusive, trustworthy.

We need to separate ourselves from hatred. It is an abstraction that potentially could destroy the human race. And you and I are not abstractions. We are real people, living in a real place, doing real, productive things.

And that is where we must keep our focus—on the practical reality of life. And on the everpresent reality of terrorism. For the only way to finally stop the killing is to change the way the terrorist thinks.

Chapter 2

My Terrorist

Here are some notes I made of a conversation that occurred in the Middle East twenty-five years ago. Even though I call him "my terrorist," this young man was not a terrorist. At that time terrorism as we know it was just beginning to grow. He was the best proto-terrorist I could find.

He denies that he could possibly hate himself, yet his black eyes spark as if a fire is burning inside. He says that he hates the United States. I ask him who in the United States he hates. He looks at me baffled.

I ask him to tell me about these feelings. Where does he feel hatred in his body? Does it have a smell, a color?

"I don't know what you mean."

"Well, where is it in your body—stomach, chest?"

Getting angry: "I don't know. It's everywhere—everywhere!"

"You mean there is nothing left in you but hate?"

Triumphant: "Yes. It's part of everything I do."

"Well, if it's part of everything you do and think, then I would think you hate yourself."

Very angry now: "No!"

"If you are pledged to be in the service of your hate, then aren't you a victim of hate?"

Now he's got it worked out. "Yes, I'm a victim. I've known that from my birth. This is it. With every breath that I take I feel impotent. No matter what I think or try to do, I feel humiliated by the United States. Just because it exists. I remember being told as a child by my mother that the West smothered me."

I decided to approach self-hatred from another angle.

"You keep talking about how early family and school experiences convinced you that you were a victim. As you grew older, that victim-hood became impotence and you began to hate yourself to the point of committing suicide."

He settles back and let's out a relaxed sigh, "I know my mother loved me. She would be pleased if I could give my life for my people."

"Okay—that's it. It's not the modern West that is making you hate yourself. It's your mother all these years. You know what I can't forgive? Your mother has loved you, but through her own self-hated has raised you to commit suicide. That is the most inhuman act I can imagine—to raise you for the purpose of committing suicide. And for what? You won't force someone to do what you want by blowing both of you up. You and the other person are both dead. You can't get him to do what you want. What if his mother feels as your mother does, that she has raised him to be killed? What have you accomplished?

"I can't forgive your mother for that. It seems like a crime against God—Allah. Now wait, don't attack me yet. I will make a deal with you. I will try to forgive your mother, if you will try to forgive me for being a part of the modern West."

My terrorist's eyes are raging with fire, "What is forgive? Kill!"

"Well, forgive is not pardoning and it's not justifying. It's not rationalization—like, you have a good reason for killing me. It is just giving up hatred. It means *you* change, not someone else. I'm going to try to change myself so that I forgive your mother. And you should try to change yourself so you don't need to commit suicide. Do you know the Buddhists don't normally even have a word for suicide? They respect themselves.

"Well, how about it?"

He says, "I'll think about it."

I've called the young man a terrorist, but I don't believe he was organized to kill. He was someone who might have become a full-blown terrorist today. I do believe he had reached the point of hating himself. And self-hate *is* the ultimate pathology because self-hate destroys all individual experience of the *true* self. There is nothing left but an ultimate, everpresent high of self-hate. This is a psychological quality of the terrorist mind actively devoted to killing you and me.

I wish that my proto-terrorist could be saved. I think about him often, but I've lost track of him.

Why did I dig up these old notes?

I realized there was a thought that never got finished. It's a mental itch that has never gone away over all those years. Recently I read about the mother of Wafa Idvis, the young Palestinian woman who became a suicide bomber. The mother said she had loved Wafa so much and that she was proud of her daughter, and she urged other young people to be bombers.

It was then that lingering thought finally got finished. Those many years ago I should have said to my proto-terrorist, "Your mother loved you so much that she would have been proud of your suicide and murder of others? Why didn't she become a suicide bomber so you could have been proud of her?"

I wonder what he would have said to that? He probably would have been humiliated to hear these (to him) meaningless words and responded with hatred.

To get a sense of the differences between my terrorist's mind and the modern mind, imagine you and your own child in the United States. You say, "Son, I've decided that your committing suicide would be very useful in this war against terrorism. We'll show them that our young can commit suicide too." I expect he would reply, "Well, you know old people don't have the stamina to serve in an army, you would be better suited to the role. Who would suspect an old person? You are at the end of your life, and you could leave the future to the young. Also, I could use the $25,000 that Saddam pays to the families of suicides."

Chapter 3

Get Real!

On September 11, 2001, my daughter Elizabeth was coming up from the subway to go to her counseling office across from the World Trade Center. The planes had just crashed into the towers—infernos of fire up in the sky, people falling on the concrete. She survived that unthinkable day. And at the end of it, the only way for her to get home was to walk with thousands of others across the Brooklyn Bridge.

There were people of every description on that bridge. Many aimlessly dropped coats and other articles of clothing in limp piles. Women abandoned unsuitable high-heeled shoes and left them scattered across its surface. These commonplace articles had no reality amidst all that burning.

Elizabeth told how the smoke from the World Trade Towers still covered the sky beyond the bridge. People carried the flames and the stench onto the bridge with them. There was a sense that the bridge would be next. That was the reality. No one actually talked about what was happening. They felt like a band of brothers and sisters engulfed in a common, overwhelming reality of fire and destruction. Abstractions of intent or policy would only come later. Months after the catastrophe I could look into my daughter's eyes and still see that haunting reality of a world turned upside down.

If what happened that day is so palpably clear, then why is the meaning of reality sometimes difficult for us to grasp? You might say, "I can touch what's real. I'm real, my feelings are real."

When I say that what I saw in my daughter's eyes was real, I mean that I can share her reality. I can trust that it is true.

I'm emphasizing reality and trust at the beginning of this book because they are essential weapons in the war against terrorism and I will be coming back to them throughout the book.

A few weeks after the carnage of September eleventh, 2600 university professors specializing in the Middle East met in San Francisco. Listening to their comments, it seemed as though that day had never happened. It was not a reality because their minds were still in their classrooms thinking in abstractions, not in reality. They thought of themselves as having a global conversation among equals. But "equals" is an abstraction, and there was no place for abstractions in the burning reality of September eleventh. They said these were violent acts committed by individual people who were only reacting to the prosperity of the United States which humiliated them. The thinking of many of these professors was an *abstraction* of what my daughter had experienced. And their thinking in the abstract offered no way to find the reality of the hate that had changed our world.

I'm proud of my daughter. She could go through the terror—the fear and the uncertainty of what was happening—yet still grasp the reality that these terrorists were a small segment of the Islamic people.

Islam is made up of many human beings. What is the reality? Is it a religious abstraction or is it living, breathing humans, each unique in all their diversity? Shiite Moslems in Iran are different from Sunni

Moslems in Egypt. Secular Moslems in Turkey are different from fundamentalist Moslems in Saudi Arabia. But does each one's reality depend more on being a religious abstraction or on being a human being?

All of us need to get real and experience the world as it is—keep our eyes on the ball. Abstractions will not help us to do that. Abstractions will only distort reality. We *must* get real to fight terrorism.

There is more to this war than killing Osama bin Laden. To wage this war, you and I must fight hatred. For that we need to use tools and weapons different from those of traditional warfare. To do that, we need to feel clearly the reality of how the terrorists hate.

ISLAM

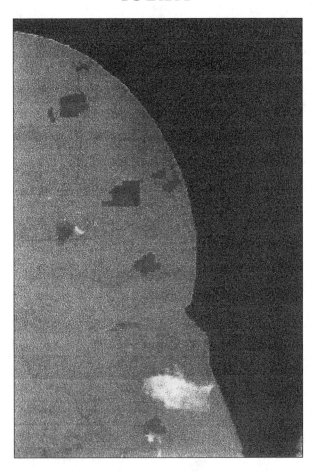

II

Nurturing Hatred

Chapter 4

Pakistan

I'm going to take you on a quick trip through the changing realities of the Arab Moslem world during the last twenty-five years—a trip that will unveil why, when, where, and how self-hatred has been bred.

Moslem countries have spread around the world, far beyond the Arab race. They are different in race and physical circumstance—from arid desert to lush tropical forests. But they have all experienced terrorism just as the countries of the modern world have.

Looking back, I see a turning point in 1977. The Islamic world entered a twenty-five-year period of change marked by a growing hatred of modernity that eventually erupted in the attack on the World Trade Center. It was not just external things like modern dress and cars and buildings that changed, but thinking changed for many Moslems during those twenty-five years to exclude any ideas that did not stem directly from the Moslem faith. Still, a large number of Moslems wanted to live with modernity, but did not think it wise to say so publicly. Their Moslem faith had not diminished, but they could be ostracized or killed for being modern.

I was in Pakistan at that time, working as a consultant for Ali Bhuto, the democratically elected president. I was trying to figure out how the minds of the Pakistani farmers worked. The United States had delivered newly engineered wheat seeds that were supposed to revolutionize crop yields in arid northern Pakistan. Bags of the wheat seeds were shipped to warehouses around the country to be given to the farmers. But the farmers wouldn't use them.

We sent troops to the warehouses with orders to guard the seeds until a different use was determined. Before we knew it, the warehouses were empty, the soldiers were richer, and the farmers were planting the seeds. The poor, oppressed farmers could find the money to bribe the guards to let them carry away seeds. No matter how poor a farmer is, he finds value only when he can buy the seeds. Then he is not humiliated.

I told this story to a Pakistani recently. He snorted and said, "Nothing changes." Perhaps the minds of the farmers haven't changed, but the thinking of most Pakistanis has changed drastically. Now they see themselves as victims, as being humiliated.

One day as I made my way to the office building where I was working on an agricultural program for the whole country, I remember stopping by a ten-story, Western-style building. Looking down the street, I saw men in Western suits. Women were wearing Western dresses. They talked to me like Moslems aware of the advantages of modernity. The cars were familiar Fords, Dodges, and Cadillacs. The people here were coming to use modern thought. They were finding the freedom to think in ways they had never dreamed of before. Their futures held exciting possibilities.

I also recall a slightly different scene in Pakistan at that time: It is a poor residential part of town. I am standing in front of a mosque. It is the oldest mosque in the city. It is one story with a flat roof and white-washed walls that extend beyond the building to enclose a large courtyard on which the mosque opens. The yard is sand, and clean up to the walls. There is no fountain or art. I venture in. I had wanted to attend services each day I was in Karachi. I thought this mosque would be the most authentic. I didn't stop to realize that no upper-class Pakistani would be found dead here. Everyone here was in thin, washed-out white robes with open sandals. I crept into the mosque, took off my shoes, and knelt down, bumping my head on the floor and sitting up when everyone else did. I knew "Allah Akbar" and a few other prayers. I noticed my presence caused some disturbance, but I left unharmed. After a few weeks of daily worshipping I felt accepted, but then one day when I left the mosque the people of the congregation didn't leave the courtyard. When I tried to slip out I was stopped. I found myself crowded into the middle of the courtyard, and everyone was looking at me and shouting. A man waved a book in my face. I could see it was the Koran.

There was a disturbance at the gate which rippled slowly in toward me. Finally a young boy came forward from the crowd. He said, "Sir, I have been to school where they teach me English. My family here and all these other people are very poor. We appreciate your coming to our mosque. We have collected enough money to buy you this used copy of the holy book. And we hope you will take it and use it and continue to learn from it."

Now I could see that the man with the book was trying to hand it to me. I took it and a large sound went up from the crowd. My eyes still water as I write this down. I felt absolutely safe and secure. Despite the fact that I was a foreigner, there was a bond of trust. I'm sure there were no terrorists at that mosque. They were good people.

I was going to work one morning after that, walking down a small side street. As I turned the corner to the office, I saw the windows of my two-story office building were broken out and the door was hanging on one hinge. Papers were strewn out onto the street, and there were no sounds. I noticed there was no one on the street. I turned in the opposite direction and found a cab.

I pulled all my Pakistani money out of my wallet and gave it to the driver. "I want you to take me to the airport but not by the highway. There may be road blocks."

The driver seemed to know me. Was he from the mosque? He said, "Yes, you leave."

I left everything in the hotel room, including my treasured copy of the Koran. We took off down side streets. Soon we were into a narrow street with three-storied buildings on each side. Doors opened directly on the street. There were no cars, lots of people, and some donkeys. I was surprised to see rugs in the street; we were driving right over them.

The driver said, "They no mind. Make new rugs and put in street for people walk on. Good for rugs."

I got a flight out of the airport, my mind filled with the street of the rug makers. I still remember it vividly. It was as though we were standing still and the carpets were carrying us along with smells of wool and the guttural sounds of the Arabic comments.

I learned later that the military of General Zia had overthrown Bhuto that morning. He was killed. That was the end of modernity in Pakistan. My new Koran reminds me of a world that might have been—a dream and a hope.

In 1977, women were wearing mini skirts, not veils. Today, some twenty-five years later, the same street that had been filled with western-dressed, productive people is clogged with a mob of men in turbans and long white robes. They are shouting, "Death to the United States!" and "Down with the murderers of innocent Afghans!" The shop keepers aren't necessarily buying this, but they're not objecting either. The same building is there, but it is now so trashed you would hardly recognize it.

Saudi Arabia has funded new mosques, and their religious schools have spread across Pakistan. The teachers and imams are fanatical agents of a conservative view of the Koran, which excludes the possibilities of modernity. The army and intelligence sections of Pakistan are natural allies of the teachers and imams. I blame the army (the Saudi cabal) for the death of Ali Bhuto, the only great leader Pakistan has had.

Trust is gone. Safety and security are gone. Osama bin Laden T-shirts are everywhere. His image seems to shriek, "If you see an American anywhere at any time, shoot him down!" Young children about the age of the boy who translated my gift of the Koran rush along the streets carrying sticks. They pretend they are beating Americans to death. They sure don't know how to speak English as the young boy with the Koran did twenty-five years ago. I still read my Koran and learn from it. I pray that my young boy did not become a terrorist. I believe that a large majority of Pakistan's people still yearn for modernity.

Today I know a young Pakistani intern working in the United States to become a doctor. He comes from a wealthy Pakistani family who left Pakistan during the years of terror after 1979. He was raised in Paris. However his family has now returned to Pakistan. His clothes are elegant.

I asked him once, "Do you truly love the modern world, with all the diversity and competing faiths?"

He answered, his face full of joy, "Of course I do. It is everything to me. There is room to grow."

"Well, how do you feel about Osama bin Laden?"

This time his face was full of exultation, "I love him. He is the incorruptible knight in a corrupt world. You will never kill him."

"I'm confused, those are opposite feelings. How can you feel both in one body?"

His face flushed, "Well, I *can* feel them both." Then he walked off.

Perhaps the ability to weigh those opposing feelings is what we need in Islam and in the modern world in order to live together absent the terrorist mind.

Chapter 5

Iran

Iran is west of Pakistan across Afghanistan. I'm not going to discuss Afghanistan; you know as much about it as I do. Iran was even more modernized than Pakistan in 1977. With the support of the American and British governments, Shah Pahlevi ruled from the Peacock Throne. The people of Iran were Shia Moslems but were also Persians with their own language and a conviction that they were superior to their neighbors. (Remember the book, *The Rubaiyat* by Omar Khayyam? It was very popular in the United States at that time.)

The majority of Iranians were comfortable with the Shah's rule. Their prospects for open, inclusive, westernized thinking were close to realization. Groups of young girls educated in Western thinking would skip along wide avenues in Tehran. Then, suddenly, it was as though night came, but the sun never rose again. The new way of thinking was exclusive. Love, hope, and dreams of a productive future disappeared. How could such a complete mental reversal happen so quickly?

What happened was that in the revolution of 1979 the American and British governments did not support the Shah, and the French allowed the insertion of the Ayatollah Khomeini along with an Islamic theocracy to govern Iran. Western thinking was anathema to the Moslem clerics, since it was inclusive of diversity of thought—a mental chaos compared to their version of the closely controlled and exclusive Moslem religion. The United States' betrayal of the Shah was understood in the Islamic world as a defeat of the Great Satan, so rich and fat and weak.

I graduated from Princeton University's Woodrow Wilson School of Public and International Affairs and have remained an active alumni. I recall a radio program in 1979 during which Bernard Lewis, a distinguished Princeton professor of Middle Eastern studies, had asserted that the fall of the Shah would not lead to freedom and prosperity but would presage a loss of freedom and productivity. People didn't understand, he said, that the Moslem religion was a set of rules and penalties that took away freedom and placed governing power in the hands of fanatical religious rulers. Women would suffer the most.

Many Princeton students organized protests against his speech—too reactionary they claimed. Well, Professor Lewis was absolutely right. Everything he predicted came true. Now he has written an excellent book, *What Went Wrong*. It tells about the cultural clash between Islam and modernity. It has also been a national bestseller. I recommend it highly.

Hesbollah was formed as Iranian terrorist cells in the Bekaa Valley in Lebanon. The Lebanese capital, Beirut, rose up from the Mediterranean Sea. It was a pearl of French colonial architecture. But during the 1979 revolution, Beirut became a hell of bombings and assassinations. American CIA agents were captured, tortured, and killed. I had been in Beirut shortly before this mindless destruction descended upon it. It was a culture inclusive of all nations, not just the Middle

East. Rich people came to retire there. The American University there was the most famous in the Middle East. But it was not immune to the Iranian terror.

Then came the terror of holding hostage the American Embassy in Tehran. The embassy was an outstanding building, and to the Ayatollah it was a symbol of the chaos of the Western mind which they had defeated. Our tragic, failed attempt to rescue the Embassy hostages was an even greater defeat. Then the Marine barracks in Lebanon were bombed. President Reagan withdrew our troops. Suddenly a fundamentalist Moslem religion was in charge of the Middle East.

In the 1980s there was evidence of a growing erosion of an Islam that included modernity. Fundamentalist Moslems excluded modern thinking, and they were gaining control.

The Ayatollah Komeini declared he would create a docile Moslem society of young people and decreed that everyone have more children. His mistake was that he did not teach hatred sufficiently enough in the schools. Now these young people are becoming more interested in modern ways. They describe religion as a tool of repression. Religion keeps boys from talking to girls. Girls are told to cover all their hair because hair is immodest. If they organize to protest, they may be tortured or beaten.

Most Moslems are not fundamentalist. Many left Iran, but their faith in the Moslem religion was just as strong as anyone else's. Today many refugees have returned to Iran to live peaceful lives.

Did you know that Chanel hand bags worth a thousand dollars each are currently produced in Iran? The Iranians have always thought of themselves as being Persian, not Arabian. Persia's culture is old, older than Greece. They ruled a large part of the ancient world. When Arabia was ignorant tribes, Persia was rich and cultivated. Iranians had the self-confidence to believe they could take on Western business and come out the winner. This self-confidence does not represent the Ayatollahs, but rather is called Iranian in the street.

In Iran they have translated my book, *Beyond Literacy*, which won the Benjamin Franklin Award for the best nonfiction literature in the United States. The translator, talented, MaryAm Kany, has become a close and dear friend of mine. We laugh over the problems of translating my very personal style into Persian and the problems of living peacefully in a very fundamentalist country.

Chapter 6

Iraq

We have been looking back twenty-five years to understand the beginnings of the terrorist mind. However, the mind of Iraq presents a special case; in this instance we must look back some fifty years. At that time I was a staff correspondent for the United Press. In 1948 the United Nations had just authorized a state for Israel, and Israel had declared its independence. In 1949 Iraq, Syria, Lebanon, Jordan, and Egypt gathered their armies and together descended on Israel to erase it from the face of the earth.

Iraq and Jordan both had British-trained armies and heavy equipment. The odds were overwhelmingly stacked against Israel. Jordan had already controlled part of Jerusalem, Iraqi forces were attacking the old Jewish section of Jerusalem, and the combined armies successfully took over the whole city. There was one story that made a lasting impression on me. Here it is.

An Iraqi army officer, spiffy in his British-designed uniform, picked his way among the rubble of houses and approached a small, barely standing structure. He knocked on the door. A voice invited him in. He found an old, bearded Jewish rabbi working on his papers.

"Rabbi Buber," the Iraqi officer said, "I know you are a world-famous philosopher and revered by all faiths. Your work is important to all nations. But we are destroying this Jewish section. I can bring some men to move you and your things to safety."

Martin Buber looked back at him with luminous eyes of seemingly endless depths, "Thank you," he said, "but I am with God."

The Iraqi officer left, feeling that he, too, had been with Allah/God, and wondering if perhaps these Gods were all the same. In any event, the following day he managed to destroy the old Jewish community and left Martin Buber's house standing.

You should know that this Iraqi was an educated man who revered the finer things in life. He embraced diversity without hate. He was the kind of Islamic man we need to help us in our fight to be free of terrorism. Perhaps he is still alive in Iraq today.

The Jews pushed out of Jerusalem, took to the hills, and continued sniping at the invading armies as they could. In an unbelievable military miracle, the Jews managed to prevail and retook all of Jerusalem, including the area owned by Jordan. Iraq retreated from the West Bank, leaving it in Israeli hands. Israel pushed to the Red Sea in the south, carving out pretty much the boundaries we see today.

For the Iraqis, the shame of their retreat had little to do with Israel. It had everything to do with losing a war they should never have lost. They had betrayed their religion and their understanding of themselves.

Now let's look back even earlier, to 1939, and the beginnings of World War II.

The British had been the protectors of Iraq since World War I when, allied with Germany, they had defeated the Ottoman Empire. Iraq came into existence because the invincible Ottomans lost. Under that Empire, it had been a neglected province, but under British control it became the nation of Iraq (*Iraq* could mean "the cliff" or "the sea" in Arabic). Though still somewhat neglected, the British tried to establish a model of their own government there with a Hashemite line of monarchs presiding over a democratic government. The British trained a fine Iraqi army and gave Iraq its independence in 1939, keeping only a few bases there.

At the outbreak of World War II, the Iraqi government secretly supported Germany; eventually it found a way to declare the country an ally of Germany. Iraq never practiced Nazism; what was significant for the Iraqis was that the Nazis were killing Jews, and even more important, they were winning the war. They had seen the Ottomans lose, and they believed the Iraqis could win. The British had only a few troops at the air base they had maintained during Iraq's independence. The entire Iraqi army concentrated on the British base and suggested that they surrender. The British commander of the air base sent out his troops. They outfought and outmaneuvered the Iraqi army, retook the country, and formed a new government. The new government supported the Allies against Hitler. The Iraqis had lost again.

I am not suggesting that the Iraqis were bad soldiers. They were not. But they were an extreme example of modern Islam. Their ancestors had been Mohammed's soldiers—armed with a sword and a lance, and living off the land, they had conquered most of the known world. They were armed missionaries. They didn't lose.

Iraqis couldn't believe that they could lose. They were a conquering race destined by God to rule. But they had lost over and over again during their fifty years as a nation. In 1967, the same array of nations that fought the 1949 war (Iraq, Syria, Lebanon, Jordan, and Egypt) again did battle with Israel. It only lasted six days this time, but Iraq and its allies lost—lost again.

The British-style democracy had never worked well in Iraq. Governments changed every couple of years. So, when Saddam Hussein came to power in 1976, he solved the problem. The nine members of the council who selected the president were appointed by him. He controlled the one-house legislature. This scenario would seem to guarantee him the presidency for his lifetime.

Then he started a war with Iran, his eastern neighbor (and his ally in the recent Palestinian wars). Iran supplied Palestinian forces with both terrorists (Hezbollah) and military equipment. The Iraqi war with Iran lasted until 1988—eight years, with millions of casualties. In the end, Saddam had to make peace with Iran with his war aims unrealized.

At the same time, he fought the helpless Kurd separatists in Iraq, even using poison gas. (Perhaps he wanted to see how it would work.) And the rest of the world did nothing. Today the Arab League has sworn to stand firm together and resist if the United States attacks Iraq—the very country that had been invading them.

Then Saddam launched his famous attack on tiny Kuwait—and won! For the first time in their history as a nation, the Iraqis had won. Kuwaitis were massacred, buildings destroyed, and Kuwait's oil fields set on fire. The average Iraqi citizen must have been elated to have won at last.

Saudi Arabia would be next, and the Saudis knew it. However, Saddam must have known that an alliance was gathering its forces to attack him. How did he think he could possibly have resisted them? Of course he lost in a few days—lost again! Five wars lost in fifty years!

The experience of Iraq should serve as an example to the Mid-eastern countries. Moslem warriors never lost wars. So Iraq's only explanation was that these were not lost wars, but only temporary setbacks. Even if it takes another thousand years, Islam will rule the entire world, and unrepentant infidels will be slaves or be killed. It is little known that after the Gulf War of 1991, high-ranking U.S. army officers received permanent death threats. "We will get you sooner or later. You will never again be able to rest easy." President Bush himself, in Kuwait after the war, narrowly escaped assassination.

The final terrorist weapon is the suicide warrior who will always kill many more people than himself or herself.

But don't forget about the Iraqi army officer and Martin Buber in the 1949 war. Also remember that Iraq has a secular government, an educational system, and literary prizes. These are the envy of Islam. Most Moslems are not Wahhabi-dominated fanatics. In the present world atmosphere, however, they do not feel it is safe to speak up. But we can reach them by using some of the suggestions in this book—heal hatred, include rather than tolerate, offer mutual trust, support literature and literary prizes, appeal to our common humanity—one person at a time.

Chapter 7

Egypt

Egypt is a different story. Twenty years ago it was close to the United States and the Western mind. President Sadat had made peace with Israel. He was assassinated by Moslem terrorists, and then Mubarak became president. In a little-known campaign, the government security forces tracked down the terrorists and killed them, much as we are doing in Afghanistan today. For many years Egypt continued a period of peace and prosperity.

In 1988 I had lunch with Madame Mubarak. We discussed her plan for introducing Egyptians to the writing of modern literature. Across Egypt, a network of government-sponsored writing schools blossomed.

That same year the outstanding Egyptian author, Naguib Mahfouz, won the Nobel Prize for Literature, a signal western achievement for Islamic literature. Let me quote his words as he addressed the Nobel Prize Committee:

You may be wondering: This man coming from the Third World, how did he find the peace of mind to write stories? You are perfectly right. I come from a world labouring under the debts whose paying back exposes it to starvation or very close to it. Some of its people perish in Asia from floods, others do so in Africa from famine. In South Africa millions have been undone with rejection and with deprivation of all human rights in the age of human rights, as though they were not counted among humans. In the West Bank and Gaza there are people who are lost in spite of the fact that they are living on their own land, land of their fathers, grandfathers and great-grandfathers. They have risen to demand the first right secured by primitive Man; namely, that they should have their proper place recognized by others as their own. They were paid back for their brave and noble move—men, women, youths and children alike—by the breaking of bones, killing with bullets, destroying of houses and torture in prisons and camps. Surrounding them are 150 million Arabs following what is happening in anger and grief. This threatens the area with a disaster if it is not saved by the wisdom of those desirous of a just and comprehensive peace.

Yes, how did the man coming from the Third World find peace of mind to write stories? Fortunately, art is generous and sympathetic. In the same way that it dwells with the happy ones, it does not desert the wretched. It offers both alike the convenient means for expressing what swells up in their bosom.

In this decisive moment in the history of civilization it is inconceivable and unacceptable that the moans of Mankind should die out in the void. There is no doubt that Mankind has at last come of age, and our era carries the expectations of entente between the Super Powers. The human mind now assumes the task of eliminating all causes of destruction and annihilation. And just as scientists exert themselves to cleanse the environment of industrial pollution, intellectuals ought to exert themselves to cleanse humanity of moral pollution. It is both our right and duty to demand of the big leaders in the countries of civilization as well as their economists to affect a real leap that would place them into the focus of the age.

In the olden times every leader worked for the good of his own nation alone. The others were considered adversaries, or subjects of exploitation. There was no regard to any value but that of superiority and personal glory. For the sake of this, many morals, ideals and values were wasted; many unethical means were justified; many un-counted souls were made to perish. Lies, deceit, treachery, cruelty reigned as the signs of sagacity and the proof of greatness. Today, this view needs to be changed from its very source. Today, the greatness of a civilized leader ought to be measured by the universality of his vision and his sense of responsibility towards all humankind.

Does he mean that we need a civilization that includes all nations and religions, such as the United States, or does he mean that the Moslem religion will conquer and rule all? In any case, now Madame Mubarak's schools are under attack by a new wave of terrorism and Naguib Mahfouz has been stabbed by terrorists. Authors have been assassinated, and many more threatened.

Egypt's government had the will to kill the terrorists who assassinated President Sadat. It does not seem to have the will to kill terrorists who assassinate writers. Yet the literature of Egypt may be as important as a president, no matter how great a president he was. We will have to see how it goes. Literature that expresses both Islamic and modern thought presents a fundamental way to find peace.

Mahfouz rationalized the terrorist mind and yet was the target of terrorist assassins. He didn't support terror enough! How much is enough for the terrorist mind? Is there enough?

Chapter 8

Saudi Arabia

The Saudis have been the economic leaders of a great world revolution in the Moslem religion over the last twenty-five years. They say they are just following their religion like everyone else. But the practical reality is the rise of terrorism.

We could lean on the Saudis to modernize their schools. But I can hear the Saudi response, "Oh, we are just teaching the bible (Koran) to these sweet children. How could anyone find fault with that? It's just like your missionaries." That's fine, but their education turns out terrorists. Their bible says everyone not a Moslem is the enemy to be conquered. (Remember that the only Islamic country that was not conquered by arms was Indonesia.) We don't even have the means in the United States to keep Islamic schools here from teaching terrorism unless we change our laws and our lives.

Significantly, the Saudis are beginning to worry about the possibility of running out of money. They pay their citizens to live and follow the Koran faithfully. With nothing to do through the long, hot days, and keeping their wives (however many they have) as slaves, what do you think is going to happen?

An increase in population, plus the cost of proselytizing the Islamic faith, minus the competition from other oil-producing states could leave the Saudis strapped for cash.

Thomas Friedman published a marvelous article in *The New York Times* on Easter Sunday (2002) in which he pointed out that the significance of the suicide attacks on our Trade Center towers was that they were a suicide attack on a country whose citizens worship life—we don't want to die and we don't want other people to die.

Palestine is such a small country, only three million people. The town in Texas where I live has more people. You could walk across Palestine in a day. It doesn't produce enough to take care of the people who live there. It is not a place of literature or learning. Yet the world seems prepared to use it as a battleground to thrash out old issues that have become meaningless today.

Europe seems to use Palestine to confront the Israelis. There is a great, unspoken feeling of guilt in all of Europe over the Holocaust. Palestine is a way of confronting Europe's feelings of guilt with the current issue of conflict between Israel and Palestine. I know that European human rights groups will deny their unusual interest in tiny Palestine as a resolution of the Holocaust, but it's something to keep in mind as the war in Palestine plays out.

The United States and England must now confront their roles in the creation of Israel in the first place. Islam must have feelings of guilt about keeping Palestinians isolated in camps through these generations. Also, it seems that Moslem fanatics see this as a threat to the anti-modern revolution they have been winning in the last twenty-five years. They must be seen to win this war with Israel to keep their revolution going. There are so many players in this pot, all with different motives.

It reminds me of the Spanish Civil War, in which differing antagonists in the world—the Nazis, the Communists, the Lincoln Brigade of the United States—were using World-War-II tactics and tools. The poor Spanish people suffered the most—and please remember that it didn't matter in the end who won. In the present, the poor Palestinian people suffer the most as others work out their own problems. Who finally wins in the end, Israelis or Palestinians, will not seem important twenty-five years in the future.

What will be of importance in the future will be the tactics and tools developed during the Israeli/Palestinian war. The most obvious tactic, of course, is suicide bombing. To grow a crop of young people to become martyrs takes about fourteen years. And the indoctrination coming from many people takes time.

In Saudi Arabia, women with American citizenship are held hostage and the State Department refuses to be concerned. In Operation Desert Storm, U.S. troops saved the Saudis' bacon. Later the United States marine barracks in Saudi Arabia were bombed, and the State Department did not follow up. American women soldiers are treated just like Saudi women—they are subjugated—and the U.S. government doesn't respond. Now the Saudis are denying us the use of our billions of dollars of Saudi bases if we attack Iraq. Again, there is no response by our government.

Just a word here about Saudi Arabia's neighbor, Iraq: From the point of view of the terrorist mind, Iraq is the opposite of Saudi Arabia. The distinction is important. Iraq does not export fanatical terrorism to other countries beyond Palestine. The Saudis have long exported and continue to breed terrorism throughout the world. Both Saudi Arabia and Iraq support suicide bombers in Palestine, and Iraq used rockets to bomb Israel during the Gulf War. But those were the actions of one sovereign state against another. Iraq may be taken out militarily, but that will not affect the war on terrorism. Iraq is drawing a nationalistic image of the United States as the enemy. It is not breeding terrorism. Saudi Arabia has been, and will continue to be, a natural enemy of Iraq, but it acts as though it were more an enemy of the United States than of Iraq.

Chapter 9

Palestine, A Sad Story

This story is not about Israel, but a little history is in order to tell about Palestine.

In Israel in 1985 I found cause for hope. Negotiations were going on which would result in the Oslo agreement—land for peace. I was in Israel at the time, consulting on an anthropological find.

In those years I found peace in Israel. I could drive anywhere through the West Bank feeling perfectly safe and secure. Palestinians were open to inclusive thinking. There was hope for a modern future. But today we all know of the Intifadas and the battlefield that Israel has become.

Fifty-six percent of the Israelis wanted to give Palestinians most of the West Bank in negotiations proposed by President Clinton. After Arafat rejected those proposals, the present Intifadas began. Today, fifty-three percent of the Israelis still feel the same way.

The *reality* of the Intifadas is that they have been pointless. But no one has looked at the practical reality. The Palestinians are unable to comprehend that their experience of life on the West Bank has gotten worse, and the Israelis are not able to understand that decades of war have not changed the point of view of Islam. No one can win.

Alan Dershowitz, the famous lawyer, has said that we can solve this problem by never giving the terrorists a reward for any act of terrorism. This seems to make sense, but, as we have seen in Palestine, it doesn't work. That's because Palestinian terrorists view their actions in an abstract, rational way. Their intent is to commit unspeakable horrors on innocent civilians—both their own and Israel's. And they continue to accelerate their terrorism.

There is only one solution: The reality that steers the terrorist mind must change. Only then will the actions of these terrorists change as well.

One of the great Islamic writers of our time is Rajah Shehadeh. Those of his books that have been translated into English are listed in the appendix. In his latest book, he describes the life of his father, Aziz Shehadeh. I'm going to relate a fragment of Rajah's story of his father's life in my own words. If I could have known him, this would be a better book. Unfortunately, he was killed in 1985 when I was in Israel.

Aziz Shehadeh was a prominent Palestinian lawyer living in Jaffa. According to the United Nations plan, Jaffa was going to be part of Israel. In 1948, the Palestinians attempted to take the land given to the Israelis by waging war. The Israelis were about to win. For protection, Aziz took his family to Ramallah in the hills of Jordan, forty miles away.

Twenty years passed. Aziz would go up on the roof of his house and gaze across to his beloved Jaffa on the waters of the Mediterranean, but he was in a different country now—Jordan. As the years passed, he watched the lights of Jaffa grow brighter and expand along the sea coast. He was happy to see the old colonial town prosper.

Then the war of 1967 broke out. The Moslem countries of Jordan, Syria, Iraq, and Egypt, acting together, planned to ambush Israel with the intention of obliterating the Jewish people and their country. The Egyptian general, Hakim Amer, said in 1967, "Soon we'll be able to take the initiative and rid ourselves of Israel once and for all." The West Bank, which belonged to Jordan, was the key to the ambush. If you recall the maps of Israel, you can see that the West Bank was a fist plunged into Israel's side. But Israel was an inclusive, modern country, fighting an exclusive Moslem people. Israel was left in possession of the West Bank.

This seems analogous to the French possession of Alsace/Lorraine taken from Germany in war. Most of the people still speak German and have Germanic ways of living, but they don't think of terrorizing France.

One night after Israel won the 1967 war, an Israeli lawyer friend of Aziz came by and asked if he could help in any way. Aziz wanted to be taken to his old hometown, Jaffa. His friend said that he would be happy to do that. Aziz walked through the streets of his old hometown. They were just as he had remembered them, but the streets were dark. His friend said that he would like to show him Tel Aviv just down the coast. As they approached, lights were blazing as far as the eye could see. It was a big cosmopolitan city. His friend showed him the opera house, the museums, and the public gardens. Aziz was overwhelmed with such a vital, vivid scene of city life, something that had never been in this land before. The final blow was the realization that these were the lights he had been watching from his rooftop in Ramallah all those years, thinking they were from Jaffa.

Aziz was, and remained, a dedicated Moslem, but the illusion of the lights as a symbol of Moslem progress toward modernity forced him to see the reality of what had happened. Instead of acknowledging the United Nations' grant of land to the Israelis, living with it, and developing their own commerce and culture, Palestinians had plunged into victimhood. Every failure and humiliation had to be avenged with rage at a modern, inclusive society—rage turned to hatred, and self-hatred to self-contempt.

When I was in Israel in 1985, I was interested in an anthropological excavation of a cave, Jebel Qafzeh, just outside of Nazareth. It was the site of some of the oldest human remains north of Africa. The bones of a mother with her child were found in the excavation. Rather than separate the mother and child, the block of earth which contained them was hoisted by helicopter out of the cave and straight up into the sky as though going together straight to heaven.

What a shame that the people occupying that land should later stain it with terrorism. Nazareth was a largely Moslem town in 1985, clean and peaceful. There was a block of Jewish modern apartments on a rise overlooking the town, but the town itself seemed to be only Moslem. Nazareth was on Israeli land. It was not in the West Bank. Now the Moslems there are having demonstrations declaring their solidarity with Palestinian terrorism.

I used to go back and forth to Tel Aviv from the cave of Jebel Qafzeh, and once had an occasion to visit Jaffa. It was a beautiful and peaceful area at the time. I thought it a shame that Aziz had not stayed. There were so many layers of history there. There are anthropological remains at Jebel Qafzeh of modern human beings dating from 45,000 years ago. Then the Jews lived there for maybe two thousand years. After that a conquest by the Moslems put them in control for three hundred years until the Christian crusaders conquered the Moslems and ruled for two hundred years, and the Moslems under Saladin reconquered the land from the Christians and kept it for fourteen hundred years. Finally, the United Nations gave the Israeli Jews the land fifty years ago.

Aziz proposed that Moslems should accept the state of Israel as a reality and get on with life. The Palestine Liberation Authority headed by Yasser Arafat condemned him from Tunisia. As Raja recounted in his book, Aziz heard a radio message from the Authority, "You are a traitor, a despicable collaborator. You shall pay for your treason. We shall eliminate you. Silence you forever."

Aziz Shehadeh was murdered in 1985. After that, moderate Moslem leaders were gradually eliminated from Palestine. Terrorism reigned in the hearts of people intoxicated with the glory of an inevitable Islamic conquest of the world. They failed to experience the reality that this was *not* the Golden Age of Islam. Their only response was that the humiliation and impotence caused by not enough food and water, and no jobs, "forced" them to react by terrorizing innocent Israeli citizens.

I was there when Aziz was assassinated. A Hamas follower said that he was a dead man before he was killed. "He was a Moslem," said Hamas, "and all he needed was the Koran, not the stupidity of a legal constitution." "There will be no peace with these pigs of Israelis," they said. "It is us or them, and one day all Israelis will be exterminated."

The Moslem sense of *Bukhara time* indicated the extermination would happen "in the future," which means any time in the next thousand years. That is how the Palestinians can fight the Israelis. Their lack of ability to recognize the reality of their lives here and now leaves them in an abstract dream of a long-gone Golden Age when it seemed that Islam would conquer the whole world.

This was private talk eighteen years ago. The leaders of Hamas have recently made it public. Dr. Zahar, one of the leaders of Hamas, was quoted in *The New York Times*: "From our ideological point of view, it is not allowed to recognize that Israel controls one square meter of 'historic Palestine'."

Another Hamas leader, Mr. Shenab, joined in, "There are a lot of open areas in the United States that could absorb the Jews."

Do you think they are kidding? They aren't kidding. Dr. Santisi, another Hamas leader, made the most important contribution, "We are the political leaders." For them, Arafat is a loved and useful symbol. Hamas is in charge of the Palestinian people.

One of the Hamas leaders boasted that if you give him 10,000 young people, he can take out 100,000 Israelis. At that rate, it would take about fifty years to kill most of the Israelis, but the Palestinian high command has already spent fifty years killing a constantly rising population of Israelis.

If, for example, the Palestinian suicide bombers are a huge success, their attempts against the United States will be used around the world. If the war on terrorism will change the world as we know it, then this development could change life as we know it.

Today, people from both the modern world and Islam have referred to UN Resolution 242 as though it ordered Israel to return to its 1967 borders. Resolution 242 says Israel should withdraw from territories that were occupied and go to secure and recognized boundaries. Russia tried to change this to "all" territories, but was turned down. Thus the resolution deliberately referred to occupied territories but not "all" occupied territories. This gave Israel a chance to create defensible borders for itself.

The most devastating effect of suicide bombers could be control over governments. Any peace accord anywhere is at the mercy of terrorists. The terrorist who wants to avoid an accord can blow himself up. This makes someone like Timothy McVeigh seem a rank amateur.

The Palestinians can't win. None of the foreign parties can win. But no one can see the practical reality. Yet it is amazingly clear. *Just stop! The terrorist mind must go!*

Any solution is better than this madness. Each party can make out with less than they think they must have. Just stop! Surely the future of the world is more important than a miserable, meaningless, little victory either way in Palestine. If this doesn't happen, all we can do is grieve.

Believe me, self-hate did not exist in the Moslem mind 1400 years ago. So where did it come from?

III

MOHAMMED'S MIND

Chapter 10

An Interpretation of Religion

To understand the terrorist mind we must understand the development of both Islam and the Christian West. I applied to my dear friend Frederick Turner for his expertise in that area. He is the great Homeric poet of our time who has just written a book on religion, *Seven Blind Men and an Elephant, a Study in the Interpretation of Religion.* I asked him to interpret Moslem and Christian religions for me.

We met out behind my house at a place called "Cross Timbers" because here is where the Live Oak trees coming up from the Rio Grande intersect with a band of Post Oaks from East Texas. The sun is shining, and ripe pecans are dropping in our laps from the branches overhead.

Fred begins.

"Let me start with the modern Christians. In Christian terms, this is the era of the Holy Ghost."

I sit up in my chair, "Pardon me, Fred, for interrupting before you've started, but Holy Ghost? What Holy Ghost? Do you mean, like a spiritual era?"

"I mean that the history of the world must itself contain a message, a message that cannot be less than equal to the Gospel of Christ—if the Holy Ghost is indeed equal to the other two persons of God.

"If we look at that history from the vantage point of today, we notice one huge development: the astonishing progress of science, technology, and the human arts in general. That progress occurred chiefly in the parts of the world devoted to the Christian Bible and influenced by the life of Christ, while other civilizations lagged, or caught up, only when exposed to Christianity. The implication is that in Christian terms we might see progress in human art and science as the direct sign—the gospel—the very metabolism, of the Holy Ghost, the Helper."

Something occurs to me, "Fred, aren't you saying the Holy Ghost is a private religious experience where God speaks to the individual? If I accept that, a joint adventure between Islam and Modernity to understand the present terrorist's mind takes on a whole new meaning. In this light, that mutual understanding seems the only way. I find myself increasingly drawn into individual relations and noticing how today one person's experience may involve the reality of hundreds of people."

"Yes, but it originally took Islam, with its blunt insistence on the application of religious morality to public life, and its lively interest in science and technology, to rouse Christian Europe from its dogmatic slumber. Through Spain, Sicily, and Hungary came the Islamic spirit of inquiry, empiricism, mathematical insight, comparative religious tolerance, and social justice. For me, one of the most marvelous moments of human history was that time in Seville, Toledo, Salamanca, and Cordova when the brilliant young sages of Judaism, Islam, and Christianity were together laying the foundations of all the later philosophy of Europe and reinventing its art and poetry. We shall only regain the fullness of Western civilization when Jerusalem has become the new Seville.

"Perhaps the Holy Ghost was alive in the thought and revelation of Islam when it was asleep in Europe; perhaps Mohammed was indeed the greatest of the prophets. The point is obscured to us now because of the relative and temporary stagnation of Islam in the last two hundred years—strange how we always interpret the past of other peoples as if they had always been as they are now, while we accept as perfectly normal that our own civilization has gone through all kinds of changes and vicissitudes. I believe we are on the verge of a great age of Islam."

"Okay, Fred, but what about tyranny and fanaticism and terrorism?"

"Give me a little time here. Though the torch of scientific inquiry passed into Christendom, Christendom must one day acknowledge its immense debt to Islam."

I was getting irritated with Fred for not solving my problem. "Yes but you've not linked up the terrorism of a small percentage of Moslems to religion."

"Well, the Holocaust and the establishment of the State of Israel must have a special place in the evolution of God/Allah, comparable to the giving of the tablets to Moses on Sinai, the appearance of the Buddha, and the birth and death of Christ and Mohammed. The Holocaust, as the trains shuttled to Auschwitz, was a definitive sign that the universe was deeply flawed."

"That is very hard, Fred. You've dug a hole for yourself here. How are you going to get out? This way God's ethical ideas, though correct, are incomprehensible to us—but if this is so, we simply can't trust our consciences at all and might as well act completely at random or according to our own narrow self-interest." Then I caught on, "Oh, I hadn't thought of the Holocaust."

"Judaism is not just the root of Christianity and Islam and all the other traditions deriving from the Bible, but also a living religious fact in the world. Even its most hostile enemies give it an important place in their eschatology. Jerusalem is at the fulcrum of Asia, Africa, and Europe. What happens to the Jews is not just another vicissitude of history.

"God's work is severely and deeply opposed. Diabolical futures have been attacking and infecting at strategic points the stem that will bring about the divine communion. Those old doctrines, common to Islam, Christianity, and Judaism alike—as well as to many other religions—that teach the existence of devils and evil spirits, may make more sense than their cultures give them credit for. Surely we have seen the devil in the last century, have we not? What could be a clearer demonstration of his reality?

"The Holocaust now exists as an irrefutable reproach against the exclusivity of any religion. Any Moslem or Christian who continues to insist on the falseness of all other religions is relying in bad faith upon a secular regime to protect others from himself, and himself from others.

"Perhaps one day Jerusalem will be the new Seville where a single poem might be written in three languages—Hebrew, Arabic, and English.

I said, "Fred, I hear you and see how it is possible for terrorism to grow out of a diabolical exclusivity of religion. And this reinforces the evil of the Holocaust. Europe has faced the evil of the Holocaust and gone on. To anyone younger than sixty Holocaust is just a word, not the reality of a terrible evil."

"In Islam, especially in Palestine, the Holocaust has never stopped. The Germans were established as allies of Islam in Palestine during World War II. Israel is the only place left in the world, where the Holocaust, twisted and convoluted, is still an ongoing evil.

"The Jews have always been supported as conquered people of Islam since Mohammed's time. How could they now still be the victims of the Holocaust? Israel was established as a homeland for the

Jews fleeing the European Holocaust. But the Palestine Authority still teaches school children that Israel will be theirs after all the Jews have been killed."

As Fred finishes, I remember something Solzchetin wrote, "The line that divides good and evil is not a line that divides good men from bad men, but a line which cuts through the middle of every human heart."

How can the evil in every moral rule be overcome? By seeing beyond the language—the words—of the rule to reach an implicit understanding of what is real in our world. It is up to each human being to make sure that the value of life and inclusiveness outweigh hatred and the meaningless destruction of life.

Chapter 11

Mohammed's Thought

Arabs say that the Koran has no inconsistencies. That's another way of saying that it never changes. The sun rises because the earth is turning around. If something has a cause, it can be depended upon to always happen that way; it is consistent. The Koran is consistent, and it is true. That can be very comforting. You can depend on the Koran. It's about abstract reason. It applies to everyone at every time.

It seemed so to Mohammed. Abstract, cause and effect was just being developed in 600 B.C. by the Greeks, and the Byzantine Christians brought it to Mohammed out in the desert a thousand years later—just in time for the Koran. But since then people have learned to *rationalize*. You might hear someone say, "I hate the United States *be/cause* it doesn't do what I want, or it makes me feel helpless. That is misused, abstracted cause and effect.

Mohammed was born 570 years after the birth of Jesus. During his first forty years, he was occupied in various activities, such as being an administrator of caravans in the Middle East. For the next twelve years he was married to a rich woman some years older than he was. And he was visited many times by God who gave him specific directions about how people should live. During this period the religion of Islam was established. The last ten years of his life were devoted to military conquests.

His is a remarkable story. In twenty years a middle-aged Arab, living in the desert, created the world's major religion and began the conquest of the known world. Mohammed apparently believed that there was in heaven, a book, and that God transmitted that book to him during Mohammed's seizures. His secretary wrote the words down. Thus, we have a book in heaven being transmitted via Mohammed to a book on Earth. His book is called the Koran—the book of the recitation of God. This Moslem bible, unchanged today, gives the theological and moral rules, plus the civil and governmental rules, plus the punishments for breaking the rules. Especially in those early days, a Moslem had the safety and security of knowing exactly what God's rules were and what the penalties were for breaking those rules. In addition, there was a heaven where every man who could enter was promised a harem of seventy-one young, sensual women to do his every bidding. The guaranteed way to this heaven was to die fighting the infidels (anyone who was not Moslem). Apparently Mohammed did not envision any priest to run his religion. The Koran was simple and clear and covered every aspect of life. Most of the first Moslems could not read, nor can they today, 1400 years later, so someone had to read it to them. Of course it was not long before priests (Imams and Mullahs) appeared who could derive slight meanings from God's book. However, it is widely thought that the meaning of the Koran cannot be translated into a foreign tongue. Only an Arabic tongue can be holy.

Knowing something about the Arab language will help you and me. Arabic has a totally different structure than English. Arabian words have tri-lateral roots. For example "write" in Arabic has the root KTB. So "we write" is *KaTaBne*. A "book" is *KiTaBum*. A "school" (place of writing) is *muKTiBum*. You see, the Arabian language is purely logical and systematic. That is a great advantage. English is such a mish mash—the words don't mean anything in themselves. Based on logic, Arabic has been the rational language of abstractions.

Here are some English letters as they would be in Arabic: B is ⌣, K is ζ, T is ﻝ.

The problem is that Arabic doesn't include many vowels in the writing—I wnt dwn twn (I went down town.) Also, much of the shapes of the writing are decorative curlicues. If you know what the general thought is, it's not so hard.

Chapter 12

Mohammed's Army

However, Islam's greatest success was with its armies of God/Allah. Before Mohammed the tribes of Arabia worshipped pagan gods. He postulated only one God. His armies were born fighting local pagans. Islam's conquest of Northern Africa and Spain meant fighting with pagans all the way. A prisoner could join the Islamic faith and become a member of the army, or be killed or enslaved. So a small Islamic Army could become a horde. The Islamic soldier conquered North Africa with a horse, a curving sword, a shield, and a lance. Islam's soldiers were light cavalry and lived off the land. However, their most powerful weapon was the Koran. Think of what it must have meant to illiterate tribesmen to be offered a faith of one God who united them under his word, telling them what they could and could not do in every aspect of their lives, twenty-four hours a day, offering them a safe and secure life with a heavenly sensual vision at the end.

This was the scenario: The Islamic army attacked and killed enough of an opposing army to encourage the rest to surrender. Those who surrendered were given three choices. First, portions of the Koran were recited to them. You could convert to the Islamic faith. This faith was contained in the Koran. In other words, you were converting not to a man, but to a book by God. The book was clear and concise and put your actions in consistent, rational rules. If you were a soldier and converted, you became part of the Islamic army with a mission to convert the armies of the rest of the world. You could not be in the Islamic army unless you converted. If you were in a defeated army, your second choice was to die, to be killed right there. Your third choice, if you were a noncombatant, was to live by the rules of the Koran whether you believed them or not and to continue your civilian occupation and pay tribute to support the army. This missionary endeavor by numbers of people in a short period of time may well be the most successful in world experience: convert, die, or pay tribute.

Here is a brief list of Islamic conquests after the death of Mohammed in 632:

- 634 A.D. Persia was conquered and converted.
- 636 A.D. Damascus and Jerusalem were conquered and converted.
- 650 A.D. The Middle East was conquered and converted.
- 660 A.D. North Africa was conquered and converted.
- 700 A. D. Spain and India were conquered and converted.

An Arabian renaissance had begun. The Arabian language was uniformly used. It was a clear, logical language, easily taught. From 632 to 702—70 years, a man's lifetime—the religious world had been fundamentally changed. Mohammed did not envision the existence of any *states*. Mohammedans were to be ruled only by God's direct communication to each individual Moslem through the Koran.

Chapter 13

Mohammed's Rule

During those seventy years the Moslems frequently fought the Byzantine Christians. When it came time to exchange prisoners, the Moslems said, "We want the books of the Greeks. Keep your Moslem prisoners and give us books." They were saying, "We are the people of the book. We are going to lead the thinking of the world. We were created by God to use abstractions, ideas, cause and effect. Our book, our very language, is so constructed that the ignorant can become intellectual. We have been chosen to use and spread these Greek books better than you can."

That is not the way we think of Islam today, but it is exactly the way Islam was around 1000 A.D. In all the fields of classical learning—literature, math (especially math), and philosophy—they were the best.

For me, Spain epitomizes this excellence. Have you visited Spain? Take Seville, for example. The central square of the city is dominated by the huge christian cathedral. Around the sides of the square are restaurants and people-friendly shops. I turn through a small arch, then along a narrow passage . . . Suddenly I'm in a cocoon of soft green trees leading to an intricately designed palace. This is the Alcazar (*Al*—"the," *Cazar*—"castle") of the Moslems. The transition from the modern city to this place is so abrupt it seems mystical. The architecture of the Alcazar is all arches, intricately inlaid with small colorful tiles. Floors go up and down, in and out of doors, with a forgotten grace. Elaborate fountains are still playing after a thousand years. The construction was built by Jews hired by their Moslem rulers. Given that the Moslems were the masters, there was an intellectual freedom and diversity of peoples within that absolute mastery. Jews were so spiritually allied with their Moslem rulers that during the Christian–Arab conflict Jews were often massacred when the Moslem armies were defeated. It happened right here in Seville. The Christian armies were thought to have been betrayed to the Moslems by the Jews. When the Christians won, the Jews were slaughtered.

In the 1100s it was possible and enticing to see three religions here writing the same poem or scientific work in Arabic, Jewish, and Spanish.

Mohammed created the first religion based from scratch on abstract thinking, and we see the Arabs dashing across North Africa with their curving swords. They brought this way of thinking—a way of abstracting the world. Primitive people hungered for secure, enlightened lives. It worked: The Alcazars in many towns in Spain were temples to the elevated thinking of the time.

These castles were palaces of learning. The Moslem mind was a continuation of the Greek mind—abstract, cause-and-effect thinking, but without the pagan gods and goddesses of the Greeks. Mohammed's first defining war was with the pagan gods and goddesses of Mecca and Medina. If he had lost that war, his religion could not have thrived. One of the foundations of his religion was the strict ban on the pagan idolatry of art. Thus, today, 1400 years later, we still see a

Moslem art that does not show any living objects. It's abstract art. There are no idols of Mohammed in his religion.

Compare that to the Christian church at that time, its statues of Christ and the Virgin Mary, and of the innumerable saints. Moslems would have seen those as pagan and smiled at the primitive Christians. Mohammed recognized his debt to the Old Testament, but went beyond it. He wrote a testament of his own. It was not of the history of people who had guided the development of the religion. It was about the *thinking of God/Allah* transmitted through Mohammed to all the people on earth. It was about mind not history. It told each person how to think and how to act from that thinking. It was all there—penalties and rewards—no need for government beyond the Koran and the army. The Moslem religion was spread by military conquest. The Koran was an instrument of war.

But the abstract rules of the Koran were so successful that nothing changed. The centuries went by. Other parts of the world modernized and moved on, leaving the Islamic world economically disadvantaged. Nothing changed in the Islamic world. Then Islamic pride turned to humiliation. And hate appeared as the snake in the Islamic paradise. The problem was that Islamic thinking *could not* change. It was and is a great religion, the fastest growing religion in the world. But it can only offer safety and security to people who fear change. Modern people changed so radically that the Greek thinking of the Koran lost touch with reality.

Twenty-five years ago most of Islam was being attracted to modern ways of living. Both Moslems and modern people were getting together in a natural blending of cultures. It was a time when I loved the Moslem way of life—so romantic and mysterious. Then came the Saudi revolution run by the Wahhabi Moslem sect, determined to take the joy out of life.

Chapter 14

Mohammed's Iraq

Iraq has always been the land of two rivers, the Tigress and the Euphrates. Seven hundred years ago a caliph of Mohammed founded Baghdad on the Tigress River, called in Arabic, *Medinat as-Salaam*, the City of Peace. By 800, it had become the richest city in the world, the crossroads of trade routes running East and West.

But beyond its wealth, Iraq holds greater meaning for the world today. Every time you use an Arabic number, or use the decimal system, or use algebraic thinking, it originated from Baghdad. The splendor of the culture or its significance to all humanity can hardly be imagined. Unfortunately, the Mongols destroyed the city, and by the 1500s it was a forgotten and neglected part of the Ottoman Empire.

There was another city near Baghdad that was even more important to humanity. Its ruins were scarcely noticed by the Moslems, but many thousands of years ago it was called Babylon.

Gilgamesh, the mythic human, stands at the great Ishtar gate of Babylon to usher us into the human-made world—the world out of nature. But there were thousands of dark years leading up to those intricately decorated gates, gates that reached up for the stars. And early humans, like Sin-Leqi Unninni, wrote the story of Gilgamesh for us.

Here is a passage from the saga of Gilgamesh by Sin-Leqi Unninni.

> *The One who saw the abyss; I will make the land know*
> *of him who knew all, let me tell the whole story.*

Sin-Leqi Unninni retold the ancient story. He was a Babylonian priest, the same sort of scholar-priest as the Jewish scholar-priests who wrote Leviticus on their return to Israel from Babylon a few hundred years after Sin-Leqi Unninni lived. The story is about the same Eden-time told about in the Old Testament. As Genesis does, it also attempts to explain how we human beings stepped out of nature and found humanity. This Babylonian story of Gilgamesh collects many tales about him which had been told and retold for two thousand years before Sin-Leqi Unninni composed this version. Clay tablets relating the Gilgamesch saga have been found near Jebel Qafzeh in Israel, the cave I described in "Palestine, A Sad Story" as the repository for what may be the first human bones. Gilgamesh asks the first and forever-haunting human questions, "Who am I?" "Where did I come from?"

If we translate his clay signs into our alphabet, we find that Gilgamesh is called *hadi-u a-amelu*, "the man who is both human and animal." He is a double-man. On the one hand, he is conscious that his human thinking is separated from nature. The word god, *Ea*, speaks to him, making it clear that what makes him divinely heroic is his thinking. On the other hand, his double is the animal body about which his human mind orbits. It is called *lulla-amelu*, or "man-as-he-was-in-the-beginning"—in other words, an animal. For early humans to survive, they first had to make clear to themselves that they were double—human beings wearng animal bodies. Their religious rituals were making it possible to contain and bear this double knowledge.

The original Gilgamesh was the king of an agricultural city named Uruk on the Euphrates River in Iraq (in the area of our military operation, Desert Storm). Ten thousand years ago agriculture developed around Jericho in Israel with a connection to Uruk. Gilgamesh built thick walls in a six-mile circuit around his city. At the center of the city was the temple to the goddess, Ishtar. The excavated remains of these walls still exist, now level with the ground.

At the beginning of the human world, rich new farming land was being created near Uruk every day, forming the delta of the Tigris and Euphrates rivers. This new delta area was out of nature, barren of natural life, ready for early planting with plenty of water available. The first human celebration of being out of nature began here. They grew their own food and built their own habitations, creating for the first time an obsessively supernatural life.

Agriculture and female-dominated religions developed together. Women had always been the gatherers of the bounty of the earth. The parallel between children coming forth from a woman's body and plants growing from the body of the earth had been long established by the time of the agricultural revolution. The women who had been the collectors became the sowers and the planters. It was their group rituals of sexual life that became the means of giving people-as-they-were-in-the-beginning their human nature. When humans developed agriculture, thinking was selected, not the physical body.

The first art of ritual thinking was the separation of time into seasons. Time came to exist outside of the body. The second art of ritual thinking was the separation of seeds—people obsessively observing through many seasons of growing how seeds became plants that made more seeds, which were also food and could be preserved and planted at the right time to produce more food. The human-made world was in particular the woman-made world.

These two obsessive separations of thinking out of nature spread agriculture and new religions over the Middle East. From Jericho one can take the Allenby Bridge over the Jordan River and join the Jordanian highway to the remains of Uruk, the city of Gilgamesh. It is a straight shot—750 miles across the desert. The highway is now congested with trucks smuggling goods to Iraq. They are following the trail of the first human beings which leads us directly to that ancient threshold of a new kind of life.

Women were the priestesses of the agriculture which gave human spirit its final control of nature's body. They were also priestesses of the sexual rituals of the goddess Ishtar. The great temple of Ishtar in Uruk is where one can re-imagine the beginning of our religious rituals today.

They were the eyewitnesses to the advent of human mind into the world—spirit which has been contained within arts of ritual thinking ever since. All of the living of these new human beings became one integrated ritual: Agriculture was in itself an art of ritual thinking, just as it remains in many parts of the world today. Here was an entirely human, artificial place, existing out of nature. Within it, living was a ritual art from morning until night. In Sanskrit, to be *happy* means literally "place"—to have a human place.

Towns like Uruk were springing up along the rivers. Babylon was one of the cities, and it gradually drew all the other towns under its control. The Babylonian Empire, for a while, became the heart of human thinking. And Babylon, near modern Baghdad, was where Sin-Leqi Unninni wrote the myth of Gilgamesh.

Gilgamesh, while a human, at the same time needed to recognize his animal nature. The drama of this tragic wound makes up the Gilgamesh story of the wounded healer. "I saw a star fall to the earth," Gilgamesh says. It is his animal self—the wild man-as-he-was-in-the-beginning, living with gazelles and the beasts of the field. After many adventures Gilgamesh discovers that the body dies. When all of the efforts at healing and wholeness become useless, Gilgamesh at last discovers the chasm between his humanity and his animal self. "A man sees death in things," Gilgamesh concludes, "that is what it means to be human."

Thus, Gilgamesh becomes a human being. He becomes aware of his humanity unbound from the natural world. His story becomes immortal. It is his thinking that makes him human and makes us human. He is the double-man, *hadi-u a-amelu*, with human-mind and without human-mind, and he carries his double burden for all human beings. In his mythic group ritual, people could live happily in their human place because he carried their guilt of being human. His immortal self still continues. It is being passed on, and must be passed on as long as human beings are to survive.

Over Babylon on a moonless night, the sky is nothing but stars—stars piled on top of stars from one horizon of that flat, human-made land to the other. It is a living sky that pulses, reaching down. It seems as though somewhere behind all that radiance there are great wings beating.

In Babylon constellations were named for the characters in the Gilgamesh story. Under the guidance of the priests, people became aware as each character rose in the heavens at his or her time in the action of the story. So Gilgamesh was passed on through the millennia as a story in the sky. It was the first movie, and the ritual called Gilgamesh will be projected in its entirety on each and every night sky, from horizon to horizon, for as long as there are stars above the earth. Human beings have remained *hadi-u a-amelu*—with human thinking and with animal body.

When Abraham migrated from Iraq, he had to be carrying much of the Gilgamesh myth with him. Abraham embraced a Garden of Eden where the animal-born Adam and Eve became *hadi-u a-amelu*, each an animal conscious of itself, both guilt-ridden human beings. And guess who was the prophet most revered by Mohammed? Abraham.

Abraham's cultural consciousness plus Greek cause-and-effect thinking became the divine thinking of the Koran, which would, through Mohammed, help make the modern Renaissance possible. Thus, without being aware of it, the modern Western world was made possible by Gilgamesh.

The living culture of the warriors Mohammed led to conquer the world with curving swords and the Koran is like a pot of gold buried for thirty thousand years in the Iraqi desert, waiting to be unearthed. Iraq understands Mohammed's message from God because the culture of that message emanates from the very beginning of human history. Babylon was the first Baghdad. In Iraq today can be found the original human history of Gilgamesh and the original Moslem message from God. If the people of Iraq are freed from Saddam's dictatorial suffocation, they may indeed unearth that message from God—a message that can become a universal guide to Islam today.

The great city of Gilgamesh was only two miles across. Today we spin webs of thinking around the world. They began here in Iraq as human thinking.

HATRED

IV

HOPE VERSUS HATRED

Chapter 15

Searching For Hatred

Where do we look for the terrorist mind? Where do we begin? In our own minds of course. We are all human beings with the same emotions of anger and hatred. Controlling rage, hatred, and self-hatred are battles that must be fought in every human society anywhere on earth. Each individual must grapple with these human impulses. So the war against terrorism must be won by each individual, each making the effort to be a better person than she or he is today. We can begin to help each other fight hatred and terrorism by expressing the possibilities of our mutual help.

Consider the United States fifty years ago. We were actively teaching hatred about minorities, economic classes, and other nations. But individuals who saw the reality of human life waged a war against racism and changed that perspective. The fight for black civil rights in the South has been so successful that the United States now seems like a different country. That is because racial hatred is controlled by individual people.

If we look around, we see that some of the best students in our schools are Asians, that Moslems are more free to worship in the United States than in any other country, that Blacks and Moslems often find a common faith. This attests to leadership by individual people in fighting racism and terrorism in our own country.

It was not much more than a couple of generations ago that children's literature in America encouraged hatred. And in Europe the English children despised the Irish as animals, and the French children hated the Germans, and the German children knew they were of the master race. Today, there is literary room in our national identity for children of all countries to come together.

But hate is a pathology that occurs in every culture. And Freud said that self-hate is the most powerful pathology. Someone who hates himself is obsessive and addictive. Self-hate, victimhood, self-pity, humiliation, impotence—the sufferer is often unconscious of them—and can always rationalize his obsessions. Anger expressed as justified rage, repeated in never-ending cycles, becomes unjustified hate. And expressing contempt often reflects an unconscious feeling of contempt for one's self.

For example, I hate spinach. I've been saying that for thirty years without ever tasting it. My contempt for spinach has obviously become an abstraction for me. I can't know whether I hate the actual reality of the taste of spinach or not. But I get a small emotional high out of hating spinach. Or I could hate vegetables and meat and fruit and live on mashed potatoes. Most foods would have become an abstraction for me then. Hating them would give me an emotional high. I couldn't try the simple reality of tasting those foods (except for mashed potatoes) because of an abstraction that *I can't eat that food.* I am in serious trouble now. Maybe 25 percent of the diversity of my life becomes an abstraction. That translates to 40 percent of my life destroyed by abstractions about hating food. Then I could begin hating my neighbors. That would deliver a serious emotional high. Imagine, I could become addicted to an emotional high that is stimulated by hating.

Terrorists feed off of being humiliated and feeling impotent. It doesn't matter whether or not they have actually been humiliated. Impotence and humiliation have become emotional highs of hate. There are other ways of getting that high, scaling the North Face at Yosemite or sky-diving for instance. But they are real, not abstractions, so the high doesn't last very long.

Psychology describes paranoid schizophrenia as a condition in which the sufferer believes that there is a conspiracy to get him. A car parks on the street; the schizophrenic says, "See, they're spying on me." Everything in his life is threatening and humiliating. Self-hatred lives off of this humiliation.

People growing up in modern grade schools encounter students who have discovered the power of humiliating others. But most victims discover that no one else can really humiliate you. You can only humiliate yourself. A minority remain victims of humiliation and will sometimes invite it because they have become addicted to humiliation. Those addicted to humiliation include terrorists. Everything that happens to the terrorist seems humiliating. The Golden Rule is love others as you love yourself. The Terrorist Rule is hate others as you hate yourself.

Chapter 16

The Psychology of Hate

We have a small organ of the limbic system deep within our brains called the amygdala (the Latin word for *almond*). This is a source of our body's emotions.

Joseph Le Daux may know more about the amygdala than anyone else. He writes, "We aren't very effective at turning off emotions. Wouldn't it be wonderful if you did understand where your emotions were taking you from moment to moment, day to day, and year to year, and why?"

My question is, "Am I in charge of my life, or is this little amygdala, no larger than an almond, in charge?"

Richard Lazarus, an eminent authority on emotions, asserts that hatred is the body's reaction to outer events while it is entangled at the same time with abstract thoughts. When we hate, we don't want to separate the two because that separation brings us face to face with simple, practical reality rather than fueling the hatred. Can you tell if your thinking is untangled?

In my counseling practice, it is frightening to experience the deadly interplay of abstraction and self-hatred. For example, Al Sharpton learned to use an abstract idea—ethnicity—as a means to gain power. Drawing on his own self-hatred to provide abstract stimuli to his amygdala, he stimulates ethnic hatred which makes people around him almost helpless to control their own self-hatred. It is involuntary—and irresistible. Neither Tawana Brawley nor Al considered reality important. What they said became true, even when it was demonstrated to be false. Terrorists find this form of self-hate understandable. That is the way they live.

If you hate yourself, you always create a rational excuse for your behavior. Look at people who are addicted to alcohol or drugs. They have an emotional reaction to their addiction that leaves them with an emotional high. They are at an enormous disadvantage. And they can rationalize endlessly to explain their addictions.

Such rationalizing makes wise decisions impossible, so useful actions through an effort of will are impossible. Each time you rationalize, there is less reality and finally only abstraction. Thus we betray ourselves and we betray others. Reason can't disentangle itself from self-hatred because it uses abstractions, like self-hate, which can't connect with the simple everyday realities.

Along with abstraction, physical animal thinking plays a part in our thought process, too. The stimulus of a possible physical threat causes an involuntary emotional response—blood flowing faster, muscle tension increasing, sensory organs more sensitive. It is the most heightened state of being physically alive. We climb mountains, drink coffee, drive fast, to get that physical high.

Just as physical evolution is passed on to our bodies, holistic reality and abstract thinking are passed on to us through cultural evolution. In fact, we have survived as humans to the extent that our thoughts have been able to guide our bodies—especially our bodies' instinctive emotions.

So how are we to juggle emotional instinct and the reality of our lives, keeping track of them all at the same time? By discovering how to distill abstract thought from tangles with our bodies' instinctive emotional thinking. We have to focus our thinking on the real world in order to guide our instinctive thinking.

This separation of our rational thinking from our emotions is the defining difference between humans and the other animals. Humans possess an internal holistic gyroscope—a *voluntary wondering*—that points us in the true direction, the human direction. Our *human feelings* arise from voluntary thought while involuntary *emotions* arise from the instincts of our animal bodies. We must distinguish between voluntary thought and involuntary emotion before both can be lived fully—emotions in harmony with wonder, but only when the two have been separated from each other. Our thinking of wonder can guide our emotions to make our lives beautiful and fulfilling.

Chapter 17

A Community of Hate

Picture a Palestinian infant, newly born. His mother picks him up. The arms that lift him feel ill at ease, his mother's self-hate passes from her eyes to his as she says, "You are a Moslem. Allah tells you that Moslems will rule the entire world. That is your destiny." As you grow up everyone tells you that. Your mother says that you will have a chance to give your life for Allah and bring glory to your family.

All you know from birth is victimhood, self-pity, self-hate, impotence, and humiliation. In school everyone you know glorifies these feelings of self-pity. There are no differences of thinking. You grow up never having the chance to know the reality of love and compassion in the world around you.

If you grew up in the United States, it would seem that everyone had a different point of view. Your biggest problem would be including all the diverse thinking and selves around you and being self-confident that your own self existed. Because you were a growing child, you had cliques and friendships and hatreds, but there was always diversity. And as you grew you changed hatreds and cliques. But in most cases you were loved as a child without question, regardless of poverty, lack of intelligence or education, regardless of race or background.

In many Islamic states you would have only hate-bounded thinking around twenty-four hours a day. The pressure to conform would be overwhelming. In school you would learn that you must hate the United States simply because it is not Moslem and that Islam is ordained by Allah to rule the United States as well as the rest of the world. You are not told that the Moslem faith is free to flourish in the United States.

In Palestine, an Apache helicopter is circling your neighborhood, your home—a helicopter given by the United States to Israel. You feel humiliated, impotent, living in this modern world. But the Israelis are living in the modern world. How could this happen? That is the simple reality that you hate.

The school textbook tells you that Israel has no right to exist. The only point of negotiating a peace with the Israelis is to finally find yourself in a position to annihilate them. Whatever you are told you must believe, even though you may suspect it is not reality. Fanatics must always rationalize their point of view, so they learn to lie. You know deep down that you can't trust anyone, friend or foe. So you don't—can't—trust. Hatred is your inheritance.

Many modern-thinking leaders are confused about hatred fostered through educational systems. They forget that education can encourage hatred as well as eradicate it. The United Nations and modern charitable organizations have spent hundreds of millions in the last fifty years setting up schools in Moslem refugee camps. This is a perfect opportunity to teach children charity, compassion, truth, and love. Instead, the United Nations ends up sponsoring schools where the children are taught to hate. Whether children are educated is not the main issue here, but rather *how* they are educated, both in Islamic and modern societies.

Other charities pay money to local Moslem governments to *educate* Moslem children. Those children can be educated to be inclusive and caring or they can be educated to be exclusive and full of hate.

Any teacher in a United States school who taught or encouraged hatred would not be tolerated. When the Saudis pay for a school anywhere in the world they provide teachers who would be dismissed if they *didn't* encourage hate in their pupils.

Saudi Arabia is the mental and religious center of Islam. Here Mohammed was born and lived. From here his armies spread out over the civilized world to bring the Moslem religion to the conquered peoples. Many different interpretations of the Koran developed over the years, but the Koran was so specific and abstract and unchanging, even to the end of the world, that the interpretation did not need to change in any substantial way.

The present line of rulers of Saudi Arabia followed the Wahhabi interpretation. They are very conservative and follow the Koran as closely as they can. Wahhabi imams have built the fractious tribes into a solid Saudi Arabian government. *Government*? But the Koran tells you how to live without a government. How could this Wahhabi version of the Koran be true? Of course, the Koran has always been a part of the Moslem army's approach to the world—conquer, convert, move on. It has always had a dynamic political element that has changed as life has changed.

This dichotomy reminds me of a present a lovely lady gave me twenty-odd years ago. The present was a miniature picture of a Moslem warrior from around 500 years ago. It stands about four by seven inches and has been perched on my desk all these years, supervising my activities. But it is a *picture of a person*—an image supposedly banned by the Koran.

In the 1400s, painting had reached a point in the Ottoman Empire where it competed favorably with the Italian art of the Renaissance. At that time Sultan Ahmet I ruled from his capital at Istanbul.

The British Foreign Office, in all its *un*wisdom, had sent the Sultan a huge mechanical clock. It not only kept time, but had life-size figures that came out of the clock and danced in perfect rhythm with the encased music. The implication to the Sultan was that the British could make people. After suffering with this thought for a while, the Sultan decided this was blasphemous. That he was right. The British were indeed infidels! The Sultan is reported to have taken a heavy hammer and destroyed the clock, then went on to declare that further painting was banned and that Moslem artists could design rugs with no depictions of living things.

So the Wahhabis are correct in banning all pictoral art. But the ban is just a few hundred years old. It doesn't represent the rich, wonderful diversity of human beings living the Koran.

More important, Wahhabi teachers and ministers staff the Saudi government and the Wahhabi mosques all over the world. They call their schools Madrassas. They teach hatred to children and adults rather than the rich history of the Moslem faith.

Billions of dollars of Saudi money have gone into the mosques, schools, teachers, and students. Where does the money come from?

The money comes from the United States oil companies. They pay the money to Saudi Arabia for their oil. The Saudis take the money and buy schools and mosques all over the world and pay for the Islamic preachers and teachers to bring the Wahhabi message of hatred. This has been going on for more than twenty-five years.

Stephen Schwartz says that 80 percent of the mosques in the United States are Wahhabi—the same in Europe. That means we must face the fact that Moslem children in many countries are being raised to hate. Saudi Arabia is building a scaffold of hate in our country that could turn out an inexhaustible supply of terrorists from our own soil. Since September 11, 2001, TV footage shows that the Wahhabi ministers here hurriedly backing away from their previous diatribes about the United States. Do you really believe that they have changed so profoundly?

Even so, modern-thinking Islamic people withstand efforts by schools and mosques and media to entangle them in hatred and terrorism. A large majority do this very well.

The majority of the children who pass through the Madrassas do not become terrorists. Many of them grow up to be Islamic citizens of virtue and good repute who are also conversant with modernity.

Again, I think we have come down to individual cases. Each individual has been guided in different ways. This is true of students in both Islam and the modern world.

The heart of the matter is that the Arab and Western worlds are needlessly clashing. Instead, each should try to understand the other. We need both the modern world's practical reality and Islam's self-acceptance. To break the cycle of violence, both Islam and the modern world must understand the terrorist mind together. And, if we understand the reality of hatred together, we will have taken the first step in that direction.

Chapter 18

Heal Hate

Many people get overwhelmed by anger because their emotions are entangled with abstract thoughts. Their anger becomes hatred of someone or something, and finally turns to self-hatred. As part of my counseling, I have been conducting a Heal Hate experiment. This way of healing hate is successful when my clients really work at it. The experiment began twenty years ago with Miriam, a client who was flirting with self-hatred. She ran a company that designed office space and had come to consult about losing business.

She found her thinking sometimes got confused and ineffective when hatred overwhelmed her. I can see that her gray eyes are like dams—vainly trying to contain her abstract thinking tangled with hatred. This may be the key we're looking for. We decide to practice disentangling abstract thinking from anger. To do this we try to put the practical reality of thought into its proper place *between* emotional thought and abstract thought.

When her anger tangles with reason, its feeling shape often becomes a hot, transparent bubble enclosing her. She pushes on the fluid surfaces but remains a prisoner of her emotions. Can she experience the difference between her body's instinctive reaction of anger and the reality of anger?

We do a meditation in which anger is its own reality. There is no target for the anger. She moves this anger up her spine from a center in her groin, then to her abdomen, then to her chest and neck, and then to her head. Now she acknowledges the emotional high of the anger and lets it rise up through her body and out the top of her head. I tell her I can see what must be a tongue of fire flickering over her head, and she laughs, feeling some liberation. She hasn't rationalized the anger onto someone else. It is just a simple reality of her body.

Now she realizes that emotion can clean her body out, tune it up. As we talk about the problem in the following weeks, it becomes clear that anger is actually very good for her body.

Several weeks pass. We try again. This time there isn't a rationalized hatred of her customer, but pure, wonderfully cleansing, physical anger. She can feel the difference between her emotions and her abstract thinking. She feels a sense of liberation. Now she is ready to use her emotions in a positive, creative way.

She is beginning to know the difference between hatred and cleansing anger. In a few months she will manage to tune up her anger so that she is in charge, naturally balanced between physical anger and practical reality—keeping her rational thoughts at bay.

Abstract thinking can't disentangle itself from emotions. Think about when you are angry at someone. The emotion of anger doesn't last very long. You notice your anger is disappearing. What is happening? You need constant stimulation to keep the high of anger going. So you begin to rationalize your anger. "He shouldn't have deliberately put me down in front of everyone." Now your anger returns, and you begin the cycle of rationalizing to produce more emotional highs again . . . and again . . . and again. Many people reside in such bubbles of hate for the rest of their lives.

The possibility of self-hate resides in the heart of every human being. If we are going to change the terrorist mind, we first have to control anger and hatred in ourselves. You can conquer and control your self-hate with practical, realistic thought. It will give you the mental fuel you need to tune up and power your thinking.

You can't merely tell someone not to hate. That is useless abstraction. Abstractions are like rules. They are not reality. If you don't hate yourself, then you can share the feeling of living without hate with someone else. And you can make a compassionate connection with those suffering from self-hate.

I and many people I counsel practice an anger–hate exercise several days a week. If you have a structure of physical exercise in your life, you can fit in your own anger–hate exercise.

Standing straight, I begin to feel the emotion of anger in my body (not in my mind), first in my groin, then stomach, then chest, and finally head. I become alive with anger, but not anger at anyone or anything. The anger lasts for about three minutes and then fades away, leaving me alert and on a healthful emotional high.

Keep doing the exercise and it will eventually change your life, and hopefully the lives of those who fight hatred with you.

The most effective weapon in the war on terror is the practice of healing hatred.

V

A CHILD'S MIND

Chapter 19

Infancy

Whether we are Islamic, Jewish, or Christian, we all depend on the cultural chrysalis of childhood. During the first year of life, a child is a little sponge absorbing cultural feelings—feelings of hate or feelings of love—as rhythms, tones, and mental timing.

Listen to a mother talking to her infant. The child has no way of knowing what the words mean. What is being passed on are subtle energies of the past. Listen to the mother's rhythms and tones. This is how the child, born a little animal, becomes human. The mother programs its brain as her brain was programmed during childhood.

The infant begins a feedback with the human cultural continuum through mother. The mother resonates with the passed-on rhythms her infant is picking up from her and feeds them back. Thus, the two together begin the art of tuning up her infant's mind.

The meters and tones of the voices we heard as infants actually shaped the functioning of structures of our brains. That is where self-continuity comes from. Scientists are currently discovering that our brains absorb cultural continuums in the same way we absorb our parents' feelings as children.

A continuous flow of subjective energies programs your brain by changing its neuronic structures. Everyday experiences of childhood show how personal tones and rhythms are passed on by those who have lived before us. They do not originate in our brains. And even though the cultural programming of brains is most dramatic in childhood, it can happen in adulthood, and right now during our war on terrorism.

Children absorb the beat of cultural continuity. Within the chrysalis of childhood development they need an environment that does not teach hate. They need a world rich in the art of stories, mime, dance, music, and song.

Keep in mind I am not talking about young children absorbing information or rules. Rather they absorb *ways of thinking*. Their first language is babbling. They speak in rhythms of words without knowing the significance of linear sequences of words.

We may remember when we were young, playing with our toys on the floor, and hearing the sounds of mother in the kitchen and father working outside the house. Those sounds created rhythms of living throughout the day. In the evening there were quiet voices. Perhaps we were crawling around people's feet playing and sometimes standing close, doing nothing except absorbing rhythms and tones.

We yearned for the tones of our parents' feelings. Our parents passed on to us their parents' feelings and so with their parents, and back and back. Children may feel this cultural continuum as a vast womblike flow that is constructed entirely of little nonmaterial centers of living energy—subtle energies, each patterning the unique lives of particular people. They glow in all the colors, waxing and waning, and constantly shifting. There is room for everything, and there is a room for them. It is like living in a multi-faceted jewel. They can explore and visit where they wish. There are turns and crannies and depths below depths.

As adults we can return to make pious offerings and shrines so that we will not forget this immense reservoir of inner power. We draw from it to be the best that we can be.

Chapter 20

Wiring the Brain

Children undergo their deepest mental development during the first six years of their life. At birth, a child's brain cells have the capacity to wire cells together. At about one year the child has more neural connections ready to wire the brain than at any other time of life. This is true with most children. From one to six years of age they have the maximum number of connections available to wire cells together.

Let me put it this way, children inherit, through their genes, empty connections between their cells. They are like blank lines upon which they will write their experiences of reality. They have six years to use as many of these connections as they can. After that, unused connections disappear rapidly (by about 500%) over the next ten years until they reach age sixteen. At that time they will have about the same number of brain cell connections that they will have for the rest of their lives.

These are the important years; years when children think realistically. Children concentrate fiercely on the holistic thinking of reality, which characterizes the thinking of humanity during infancy.

Infants can imitate our expressions. At one year, they know perfectly well the spoken sound of "horse," even though they can't say it yet. They love peek-a-boo and babytalk; as our voices rise to a higher tone, they know we are talking to them and for them.

From birth, children wire their brains by discriminating realities, like the smell of their mother from the smell of other people. Experiments have shown that a picture of a familiar face from early childhood will cause one unique brain cell to make connections with many other cells. By four months, they know whom to trust and whom to fear. Also, by four months, they know the reality of care as opposed to neglect. Before they acquire language, they communicate with gestures—when an object is too far away, when milk is coming. These are the realities of their lives.

I watch my year-old grandchild, Cara. When her mother, Rosi, is breaking a soda cracker into quarters to fit into her mouth, Cara will impatiently push the quarter pieces of cracker away and reach for a whole cracker, which she would love to cram into her mouth. She knows for herself what is not enough and what (she thinks) is just right. These nonverbal distinctions are the realities of her life. They are wiring the connections of her brain cells. Cara uses a few words, but they are not the reality of her thinking. When she acquires a vocabulary, the words will organize her thinking, but not the wiring of her brain. The words are a means to communicate, but they are not the direct, realistic thinking that holistically creates her mind. By the time she is seven, words will start to organize the rules for abstractions by which she will begin to live.

But words do not organize her brain connections. Her brain is being wired by realities that hold meaning and relevance to her life. The reality of Cara is who she is—her self. She is already a unified person, even though that person is not readily accessible by adults. She experiences feelings that later she will describe as regret or anticipation, happiness or humiliation, love or hate.

Chapter 21

Metamorphosis

After childhood, youngsters enter a world of cause and effect where thinking is now endowed with the tools of reason to gain control over the natural world. This metamorphosis of thinking usually begins between the ages of five to seven. At this age, children since ancient times have been considered to have discernable rational thinking. The first grade in school begins at this age as does formal participation in religious ritual. It is the metamorphosis to rational thinking from the chrysalis of holistic wonder. Each person born must play out this metamorphosis of humanity through our animal evolution—when we first stretched our wings to ultimately fly to the stars.

Take a group of little children about four to eight years old. Give them each a little triangular knife edge and a block of wood. Ask them to balance the block on the knife edge. The older children will place the middle of the block on the knife edge so that it balances.

They have each emerged from their childhood chrysalis able to use the tools of rational, abstract thought.

The younger children, however, just fool around with the block, pushing it this way and that until it balances. Their thinking is still about the reality of the block.

When the children aren't looking, substitute a similar block of wood for the first one, except that this block has a lead weight hidden in one end. Now ask them all to balance the block again. The older children tend to abstract the block into two sections of equal weight. They have reasoned that the block must balance in the middle. They try and try, but the block won't balance. Some become furious and throw the block down saying that it can't be balanced.

The younger children tend to balance the block just as easily as they did the first time. Asked why the block balances in this irrational way, one might say, "That's where both sides push on my fingers the same."

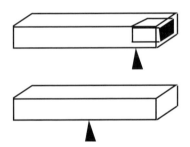

The younger children are living through the first human mental evolutionary development of realistic thought. The older children are in the later stage of mental evolution, just beginning to use the rational tools of abstraction. They have repressed their intuitive heart.

The older children have yet to discover that neither blocks nor people are really homogenous and interchangeable, that life is not an abstraction. Their newly learned abstract thinking will be useful, but it will always present the danger of becoming entangled with emotions.

As adults they can sometimes remember their lost intuitions of a pure reality.

Little children "come trailing clouds of glory" as Wordsworth wrote. Unfortunately for some of us, these intimate, face-to-face encounters remain submerged after the seventh-year development stage—sometimes for the rest of our lives. We have stepped out of a child's intuitive way of life. We feel uncomfortable—strangers cast out of paradise. Who are we?

However, in the Moslem world, Islamic thought stands ready to supply tempting rules defining who we are and what we are supposed to be doing here. And some people desperately clutch them like a drowning person clutches a life preserver, and the "clouds of glory" of their own ancient continuity fade away.

Chapter 22

Children Are the Key

Western science is just now discussing the role that culture plays in the development of each child. The human brain is plastic at birth waiting to be formed by culture into an individual adult. We know that genetic change takes eons to evolve. But it is cultural evolution that forges the mental changes that have led the modern mind to the stars.

The Eastern and Western cultural heritage goes back 30,000 years to the caves of Spain and France. These caves have never seen the light of day. They are places sacred to our human origins. One can go back into them carrying the same kinds of torches available to those first human beings. In that flickering light, paintings of animals and humans blossom from low slanting walls, their colors still intact.

Left there are hollow bones once used as flutes. Dancing foot-prints are still preserved on a patch of sandy floor. These aren't abstractions. They are facts of the art that passed on our cultural tones of thought. These footprints were made, these musical instruments were played, by living individual selves. Their lives are still with us through humanity's art. How revealing that we still go into dark places with flickering lights—night clubs and discos—to continue the ritual dances and music begun so long ago.

We have to speculate about what kind of thinking this really was. Pope John Paul called these years a time of wondering. Humans are the only animals who look at the stars and wonder.

Another description of wondering describes it as holistic. It takes in all the dimensions of real life and is reflected in face-to-face contact with voice, dancing, mime, music, sculpture, painting, and architecture.

Culture is about mental evolution rather than physical, genetic evolution. Mental evolution is revealed in cultural art forms. The mental rhythms and patterns of such art must be passed on from one person to another. By the end of the first five thousand years of mental evolution every cultural form of art had already been developed. Music, dance, painting, drama, storytelling, poetry. Even religious stories abounded to explain our existence. In that period we changed from marvelous animals who lived by involuntary instinct to a new life form, human beings. A completely different kind of thinking was added to the thinking of the chemical and neuronic structures of our brains. But this new thinking wasn't passed on through our genes. It was passed on through culture.

Through culture we shape our children to be exclusive and hateful or inclusive and caring.

Chapter 23

Women Can Heal Hatred

The abstract, authoritarian rules of Islamic thought are the rationalizations of a terrorist mind. The terrorist mind is male. Mohammed had twelve wives—Khadija, Zainah, Ruqayyah, Umm Kulthum, Fatimali, A'ishah, Hafia bin Omar, Zainab brint Jahsh, Umm Salima, Maimienah, Juwairiyah, and Um Halibah Rumlah. In addition, he had three concubines—Sabiyyah, Raihanah, and Mariyah the Copt. It may have been that Mariyah was a Coptic Christian. She was the mother of Ibrahim (Abraham), a son of some importance to Mohammed.

In a harem of fifteen wives, consider the role of the mother. Ibrahim might have had fifty siblings. He would probably have had fifteen women he considered "mother" in varying degrees. His father would have been someone he had seen briefly and perhaps even conversed with.

So, perhaps from the very beginning of Islam the bond between mother and husband and child was very different from the bond we are accustomed to in the West. For instance, the Moslem focus on women's chastity replays an ancient cultural concern—the husband's perennial question: "Is this my child?" Most wedding vows in any religion imply that God/Allah has made the separate man and woman one flesh. Children are their sanctified gift to the future of humanity.

It is easy to be scornful of this primitive male fear. Yet, even today, love includes betrayal. In fact, after thirty thousand years of worrying, at last we have the means through DNA tests to know who the father is. One poor man discovered that, of his four children, he was the father of none. If Mohammed had had this simple tool, he would not have needed large harems guarded by eunuchs.

In antiquity, the man with the most wives had the most God/Allah power over the future culture and over other men. Being educated was not most important, but the number of children of a man's blood proved his status.

If you have not seen a Madrassa school on television, imagine this one. It takes care of boys from young children to young adults. (Girls are not supposed to go to school. Men will tell them what they need to know.) It supplies lodging, food, clothing, anything boys need. Clean, well-cared-for boys sit in orderly rows reciting the rules of the Koran. Some will know the entire book by heart before they leave. But they do not necessarily know its reality—what it means in people's lives. Most have simply learned to put words into sounds so they can repeat the Koran to those who can't read. They do not know who Americans are or where they are. They have been told that Jewish terrorists attacked the World Trade Center, that Osama bin Laden had nothing to do with it, but that he is pleased it happened.

If it has not already been implanted by their mothers, here is where boys learn that they are victims. They are not taught how this came about, but only that they are victims because they are Islamic. As such they represent all of authentic and incorruptible humanity—this in itself is all they need for knowledge, humanity, and truth. In their impotence they find absolute abstract authority.

One young Moslem boy says, "From the Koran we know to hate all those who are not Moslem. America is not Moslem, therefore we hate America."

If he'd had a chance to learn more about America, he would have known that the United States includes Moslems and mosques and the same Madrassas that he is attending in Pakistan.

There are thousands of these factories of self-hatred all over the Islamic world. During the Afghanistan liberation, whenever the Northern Alliance found one of these Islamic religious schools, they would often kill everyone. They would say that the teachers and students would bite them in the future if they were allowed to live.

Hassal al-Banana in *Islam is the Solution* wrote, "It is the nature of Islam to dominate, not to be dominated, to impose its law on all nations and to extend its power to the entire planet." That vision has inspired nearly every Moslem terrorist group ever formed.

Abraham, the biblical Jew, was considered to be the common founder of Islam, Christianity, and Judaism. God told Mohammed that he should pray to the same God that Abraham and Jesus prayed to. So, presumably, he would go to the same heaven; but the Koran says a warrior dying in combat will go to a heaven in which he owns seventy-one virgins.

It is claimed by most Moslem clerics that the Koran says to look after women. They really mean look after the inmates of your harem over whom you have absolute control.

Some *liberated* Moslem men say that a woman should be able to vote with the understanding that if she didn't vote the way her husband wanted he could beat her. Today, a man still cannot even say "good day" to a Moslem woman on the street without trouble for both of them. Moslem women have always been fifth-class citizens.

And most Moslem women agree that it's all right for their husbands to beat them. A husband who doesn't beat his wife is referred to as a eunuch.

If you are a Western woman, think of 1400 years of being treated as a man treated his horse. Things haven't gotten any better or any worse. As a Moslem woman you wouldn't feel abused or mistreated. If someone came along to liberate you, you might say, "Liberate me from what? Give me the vote? That's something for men to worry about. Allow me to wear any clothes that I choose? I'm comfortable in my burqa veils."

Liberating Moslem women doesn't mean making carbon copies of the modern Western woman. What would be the most important kind of liberation for Moslem women? One would think that releasing their children to live happy and productive lives would be most important. The reality is that many Moslem women misguidedly train their children to be victims and hate themselves, so their lives become pointless and are wasted in suicide. But not all. Let us hope that enough Moslem women can be liberated to save their children. Some might wish to be trained to become a generation of teachers to guarantee that all children have a chance to live without being victims and without hating themselves and dying for nothing. They could be trained to reverse the paranoid pathology of self-hate and the impotence of victimhood.

After the surrender of Japan in World War II, we found Japanese women living as fifth-class citizens, just as Moslem women do today. General McArthur helped the Japanese write a constitution granting equal rights to women. He kept nudging the Japanese thereafter to help it become a reality.

The imams of Islam have in the past criticized Japan for becoming such a powerful society in the world while Islam remained stuck in many of the conditions of the eleventh century. Could it simply be that Japan liberated women and Islam has not? It is no small matter that Moslem women fear that being too liberated too fast may cause a male backlash.

The Moslem terrorist mind is created from a culture that goes back thousands of years and is passed on in the unconscious rhythms and tones of each child's mother. The salvation of Islam is in children guided away from hatred by their mothers. This kind of education can include Islamic culture. If women want to wear burqas, or wear any kind of dress, it doesn't matter. They can pray as they wish, believe what they wish. But we have to nudge them away from self-hate—a difficult task when all they have ever known is hatred toward women.

MODERNITY

VI

PRACTICAL MIND

CHAPTER 24

Modern Thinking

Back in Greek times, in Alexandria, Hero invented a toy that spun around through the release of steam. The Moslems inherited abstract thinking from the Greeks, so the Moslems were not able to understand the practical reality of the toy and still aren't. In modern times we were able to see the reality of the toy. We could imagine it in our inner minds and could try out various practical realities mentally before we thought of it as a motor. As time went on, the motor would run our cars and trains, even propel airplanes through the air.

Modern thinking produces this practical reality—an inclusive reality which accepts that things change and understands how things connect in the world. Because modern thinking observes how things evolve, it opens the mind to all sorts of possibilities to create new objects and technologies that work in the world of practical reality.

But in the realm of the Moslem fanatics, the rules of the Koran are always the reality, true night and day, summer and winter, 600 A.D.

or 2000 A.D. They exist for a world that never changes. If the Koran says women are subject to men, that is true. Forever and forever it is true. If the people representing the religion say that United States' citizens have two little horns on their heads and a small tail, that is true. But the rules of the Koran are abstractions. How could they always be true? In modern practicality, it is not someone's words but everyday experience that ordains the truth.

The Moslems were the world's greatest mathematicians in the eleven, twelve, and thirteen hundreds, able to express in the abstract how things connected to each other. The Moslems could have discovered the new world before 1492. They were in control of the southern half of Spain with a culture more advanced than the Christian culture. They had ports on the Atlantic and the means to create a great navy. They could have conquered the entire Western Hemisphere for the Moslems. But they didn't, because they couldn't see the reality of a new world. It had not been foreseen in the Koran. They could not comprehend the practical reality of the birth of the modern world. The minority of Moslem fanatics have still not grasped inclusive reality.

There is a Moslem saying, "Inshallah Bukhara." *Bukhara* is an understanding of time. There is the past and the present, but there is no set future. The future could be tomorrow, but it could also be a year or a hundred years from now. That is Bukhara. *Inshallah* means "If Allah wills." Thus Inshallah Bukhara means, "If Allah wills it, I will have your car repaired sometime in the next few years."

But the modern world is a web of future thinking. "I will do this in fifteen minutes, or in an hour, or in a year." We depend on things happening at the promised certain time. This modern thinking depends on mutual trust. From this very basic misunderstanding of time, modern thinking finds Moslem thinking untrustworthy and self-deceptive.

This difference in reality is the fundamental problem between fanatical Islam and modernity. Practical reality has made science and productivity explode in the Western world. A lack of practical reality has left the terrorist world unchanged. It has allowed the victimhood, the self-pity, the humiliation, the impotence, and the self-hate to thrive. But these are all human qualities that anyone could experience from time to time. It is only when they are all present all the time that we may find the terrorist mind.

To know how the terrorist mind thinks is important, but it is less important than knowing what the terrorist mind *cannot* think. If we look back at classical times, we can discover the changes in thought that happened in the West that did not happen in the Moslem world. To understand the terrorist mind, it is vital that we understand how fundamentalist Moslems and modern people think differently from each other.

Modern thinking has created every aspect of the interconnected life of the world—trains, boats, cars, airplanes, radios, telephones, TVs, computers, rockets to the stars.

Modern thinking seeks to produce people who could not commit terrorist actions on others, could not murder innocents, could not organize suicides just to kill those they hate, could not justify their lives through self-pity and humiliation.

Chapter 25

St. Augustine's Mind

You may be thinking, "I want to know how the terrorist mind thinks. I already know how I think." But do you realize that it took about 1500 years for modern thinking to develop? To understand your thinking today, you have to be clear about how that happened. You have to pay close attention to what is really going on in your mind when you think as a modern.

After my time in the Middle East, I made arrangements to go to a Cistercian monastery in the countryside outside Milan. It was located near an ancient road leading to Rome. The monastery had a good library; it would be a great help to me in adjusting to modern thought after having been immersed in the Moslem world. I would have to begin with Christian Italy in 385 A.D. in order to follow the changes in thought that have led to the present.

An outside stairway leads from the monastery's inner court up to the cells. Visitors live like the monks, with only a hard bed, small dresser, small table and chair, and a light. There is no heat, and the cold walls suck out the body's warmth. But there is a wood fire in the library. The books with old parchment pages reflect the golden warmth through the room with its low, vaulted ceiling. And the food here is marvelous, freshly grown or caught on the grounds and cooked to perfection. There are crisp, delicious apples off the trees, and the wine, fermented on-site from the monastery's own grapes, flows like water. One feels a sense of solitude and scholarly camaraderie here.

I found a shelf of *The Confessions of St. Augustine* in old calf bindings that have a deep amber glow from loving care. I'm looking for an account of his time in Milan, which was the capital of the Roman Empire in the West.

I imagine him in A.D. 385 as a thirty-year-old Roman yuppie called Augustine—that is two hundred years before Mohammed. He is wearing a tunic, tight like a T-shirt, but reaching down to his knees and heavily embroidered at the hem. He has bright green stockings pulled up over his calves, and as he walks up the steps to the bishop's palace, his yellow silk cloak billows behind him.

Ambrosius is one of the most powerful men of the Western Empire. He is in a position to promote Augustine, a newly appointed professor of rhetoric in the imperial bureaucracy. In fact, the bishop is the moderator between Theodosius, Emperor at Constantinople, and the Augustus of the West at Trier, in what is now Germany.

It is hard to see the bishop when he is not surrounded by throngs of people, but today is a quiet day. A secretary ushers Augustine through the almost empty arcades with lofty ceilings and arches and a floor of inlaid marble mosaics. The hot air ducts under the floor keep the temperature even, and running water makes a constant murmur from the fountains. They come to a small room lined with heavy drapes. The bishop is sitting on a proconsul chair looking at a book. As Augustine reclines quietly on a couch so as not to disturb him, he notices the bishop's eyes. This is the way he described what he saw: "When he was reading, his eyes moved along over the pages and his heart searched out their meaning, but his voice and tongue remained silent."

I read this sentence over and over. It is important enough for us to have a look at his original Latin.

"*Sed cum legebat* (when he was reading) *oculi ducebantur per paginas* (his eyes moved along over the pages) *et cor intellectum rimabatur* (and his heart searched out their meaning) *vox autem et lingua quiescebant* (but his voice and tongue remained silent)."

Then it hit me. Augustine thought Ambrosius was reading in a strange manner because all the people he knew read aloud. They had to speak the words in order to understand them.

It was not the sword, as he'd been taught, but the power of the spoken words that had created the Roman Empire. Through the word, mind was disciplined. The disciplined mind created law and justice. But it was *rhetoric*—the speaking of words—that created military precision and soldiers who did not break. This was what Mohammed taught.

Augustine wondered if the bishop had a sore throat or if he had been speaking so much that his mouth was tired. It couldn't have occurred to him that Ambrosius was simply, and of his own choice, reading with his eyes without declaiming the words.

Augustine was a leading scholar of his day. North African by birth, he had attended the best schools. Even so, he had never seen anyone read silently. That was his discovery, that it was possible to read silently. His words testify to a change in the nature of reading that began to manifest itself briefly in the twilight of the Classical age.

Augustine changed the way he thought, but 200 years later Mohammed didn't know that and was stuck in the way Greeks thought.

Chapter 26

Practical Reality

The subject of reality is so important to understanding Islam and modernity that it is necessary to trace how modern thought evolved. If reading silently, with the eyes instead of the tongue, was still relatively new in 385 A.D., what had reading been like before?

Have we endowed the revered figures of antiquity with abilities they did not have, those abilities we take for granted today? It does seem probable that Classical reading was used primarily as an aid to memory when making orations.

Readers must have already known the general message and read the words to check their memories. They would have read by sounding out the words and then acknowledged . . . "Oh yes, that's the way it goes." The sequence would have been speak then understand.

Today we read then understand. That is the difference.

The volume of written words that engulfs us today would have been inconceivable to Romans. They were able to read only a few books in a lifetime. Written words were rare—to be treasured, memorized, and considered carefully by speaking and savoring them. They were often run together with little punctuation, as in a phrase often found on Roman public buildings: SENATUSPOPULUSQUEROMANUS (The Senate and the Roman People). Reading this with the eyes would have been laborious. Only when the phrase is said aloud— SENATUS/POPULUS/QUE/ROMANUS—does meaning take shape. The Roman Senate and the people.

The human species developed language in order to carry thoughts and pass them on from one generation to the next. Linguistic thought developed with oral language. As words were spoken one at a time in a linear sequence, linguistic thought evolved to break experience down into separate pieces that could be strung together in the same way. In Greece around 600 B.C. abstract thinking was born, but its birth tore open the human psyche. The source of the wound was the alienation of linguistic thought from reality. This linguistic thought consisted of the pieces of reality broken away from what was really happening.

This was the scene at the advent of Christian reading, the only function of reading was to preserve oral language. It was an aid to memory. If archaic man had had a tape recorder, reading might never have developed. Archaic reading had no more thought content than a tape recorder has.

To understand the quality of this ancient reading, we can look to the development of our own children. When learning to read, children act as though they are plugged into a tape recorder. They look at the word *president*, for example, and don't know what it means, so we suggest that they sound out each syllable: "pres - i - dent." They still don't know what it means, so we tell them to say it fast: "president." Then they hear it spoken and a light dawns: "Oh! *president*." They have to hear themselves say it before they can understand its meaning. For them it is speak then understand—just as in Classical thought.

In the Moslem schools, the students speak and understand as Mohammed did—and Augustine before he learned better. There are Moslem students who read and understand, but they are still a minority. In the modern world, to read and understand is common practice among the overwhelming majority of children.

This phase of learning passes very quickly, sometimes unnoticed, but it is an example of an evolutionary recapitulation of 2000 years of archaic reading. We can still notice similar tendencies in ourselves. Sometimes while reading silently we will sound out a new word or move our lips as though we are speaking.

Silent, interior reading occurs in late childhood in the modern world. Think back to when you were young. Imagine reading the *Odyssey* laboriously, word by word, when suddenly the words disappear and you are blown by the winds of that wine-dark sea to another dimension of thought—an inclusive reality. (Such an experience could never happen with *Dick and Jane*.) You can't believe the afternoon has passed when you hear your mother calling you to dinner. Without knowing it, you were the heir to Augustine.

Beginning in A.D. 1000 there were stronger signs of interior thought. Medieval law and monastic rules began to emphasize intentionality as well as behavior. By A.D. 1200, *contritio*—"interior repentance"— was receiving more attention in the literature. One reads with increasing frequency of the recognition that sinners had thoughts. Even so, evidence of the development of interior reading was rare. Even Saint Thomas Aquinas in the thirteenth century declaimed his words in order to write them, speaking aloud until the words were polished. Only then would an assistant copy them down.

One of the characteristics of a terrorist mind is that it has not been touched by inclusive reality. This new way of thinking of reality surfaced in the Western mind after the Renaissance about 1492.

Inclusive reality is a way of thinking that pervades much of the Renaissance arts. We learned how to include multiple realities in our minds. But few Moslems have been able to do this. They live strictly by the rules which the Koran presents and exclude other realities. Moslem art cannot express practical reality. It is locked away forever from depicting living forms. What a terrible future for Moslem thought.

Within six hundred years after Mohammed, the Renaissance was upon the West. Islam did not notice. We call it the rebirth, and it must have seemed so. Cosimo de Medici was smuggling into Florence copies of Greek texts bought from Arab traders. The Golden Age of Greece and Rome was to be reborn.

But it wasn't a *re*birth. It was a *new* birth. This was a different kind of human being, capable of inclusive reality. During those birthing years, two-dimensional, flat-surfaced painting was transformed into three-dimensional perspective; science became a practical reality; the story became an inclusion of many realities.

In 1492 a remarkable concentration of events occurred in Spain. First, the Spaniards discovered new worlds—a multiplicity of new realities. Second, the first novel appeared in Spain. Novels required the reader to create an inclusive reality with the guidance of the author. Third, the last remaining Moslems were driven out of Spain. These events marked the freedom of modernity to create unexplored realities.

Fernando de Rojas was a Jew living in Spain toward the close of 1492. He wrote a play entitled *La Celestina*, which did surprisingly well. Plays had not been a big part of the past Moslem faith. Even more surprising, more people bought the book than saw the play. By reading the book, they were discovering an interior life that was not available from the immediacy of the play.

We can surely say that a new world has come. Let your thoughts have eyes, so your readers can see. Let your thoughts have ears, so your readers can hear. Let your thoughts have weight, so your readers can know the deep earth. Let your thoughts have blood and feel the beat of the heart's feelings. Let your readers smell the new world coming.

What emerged was a new type of literature through which the reader was able to internalize the words. This kind of reading was a sign of the evolution of modern thinking—but not Islamic thinking.

In the short five hundred years since the Renaissance, the novel has exploded throughout the modern world, and all kinds of people have been reading novels, imaginative histories, biographies, and essays. Such reading depends on the reader's ability to follow imaginative triggers in the prose that cause the two antithetical dimensions of thinking to *fire* together and create worlds of inclusive reality. Authors and readers of realistic writing co-invent inclusive reality. The author cannot claim to empower our creativity, for that can come only from our own mental spaces, furnished and peopled by the author's clues.

It may be no coincidence that movements to abolish slavery in the Western world coincided with the proliferation of novels. People were developing new mental room. Their perspective could embrace the personal reality of the horrors of slavery. During the American Civil War, Eliza crossing the ice in Harriet Beecher Stowe's *Uncle Tom's Cabin* became reality. Eliza and Uncle Tom became three-dimensional characters created by an interaction of readers and author.

Compare that mental quality to the Moslem mind. How many people in the great Golden Age of Islam even saw slavery as repugnant, much less tried to stop it? Among Christians, St. Paul, for instance, preached love but did not inveigh against slavery.

It is inclusive reality that has evolved, creating people with super-inclusive spaces in their minds. A new evolutionary step has imploded to enlarge our interior worlds dramatically. It isn't that we are more rational, but that we have more space in our minds to encompass and care about others.

VII

REALISTIC MIND

Chapter 27

Inclusive Reality

Compare reason to reality. When a rational sequence of thought has been completed, it ceases to exist, does it not? Like a computer, it is either on or off. On the other hand, when you read a passage that results in a vivid experience, a sense of the experience remains within you, connecting to other experiences, deepening and enriching as the years go by.

Likewise, modern abstract painting is meaningful only if it expresses a human reality. What has changed radically is the kind of thinking associated with inclusive reality in literature, perspective in art, and the scientific-industrial revolution. But how can we get a perspective on this realistic thinking? . . . Ah, perspective . . . "How sweet is perspective," as Uccello said in Renaissance times. When you see one of Uccello's paintings, perhaps you see a horse, bursting out of the foreground with men and armies gradually receding into a distant landscape. You are seeing the scene in three dimensions even though the picture itself has only two dimensions. You create the depth and the distance in your own mind, from clues the artist puts on the flat surface. This kind of picture exists *only* in your mind. Isn't that thinking process a simplified version of being lost in a book? They both become possible through inclusive thinking of reality in modernity. Don't you find that the ability to create vivid, alternative worlds in your interior spaces helps you to assess the consequences of your actions before you take them?

Even though inclusive reading has proliferated in Western culture and is irrevocably associated with changes in our ways of reading and thinking, the old Islamic abstract use of language is still with us. Remember, evolution brings along what it builds on. The abstract use of language is taking over in our new electronic information society. This information society is good for us only as long as we recognize the differences between information processing and inclusive reality.

Electrodes hooked up to your head can show brain-wave changes when you switch from reading inclusive reality to exclusive, abstract information. Reading for inclusive reality produces powerful, deep, and long vibrations, while reading for information produces short, pushed-together vibrations.

A book communicating primarily information fills us up. But when we read a reality book in which our imagination includes the art of the author, we fill the book up.

The literary development of the Islamic world is information books. Information is transmitted actively but received passively. Computers, rather than books, are its most effective tools. The measure of information is not in *meaning*, but in the accuracy of the transmission. The dimension of imagination, on the other hand, involves active transmission and active reception. The author gives artistic birth to a written possibility that the reader's imagination carries away to create his own mental reality.

Through literature, increasing numbers of people in the modern world have died a thousand deaths, lived a thousand lives. In France we have been miserable with *Les Miserables* and magnified with Montaigne. We have experienced *War and Peace* in Russia and have had *Great Expectations* in Great Britain. This common inner space is so pervasive that it is like breathing—we are hardly aware of it. Nevertheless, literature cuts through ideologies and nations, and it is saving us all.

We've had Dachau and we have gulags. What is hardly noticeable amid the noise of terrorist polarization of ideas is the quietly growing network of ordinary people including reality as a new dimension of thought. We have the mental room to create and endure common, inclusive experiences; we have the capacity for a new compassion. Inclusive reality thinking must keep pace with the information revolution.

Our purpose in following this short history of modern thinking is to disentangle the thread of explosive change in the modern world from unchanging Islamic thinking.

First, what hasn't changed? The structure of our brains has not changed radically since Classical times. What about our abstract thinking abilities? The accumulated benefits of scientific thinking have opened the universe to us, but rational thinking itself has not changed much. Pythagoras could have held his own with most of today's academicians.

In the modern world we have the evolution of a new dimension of thought. Remember in school flipping through *Julius Caesar* to pick up names and places and then creaming the test? You were using abstract abilities to comply with an educational demand for information. Then recall a time when, without educational pressure, you read *Julius Caesar* for pleasure. Without your noticing it, the printed words disappeared and you entered an inclusive world of sights, sounds, and smells. You could feel Brutus's sword shocking through Caesar's ribs and the bright blood violating the white marble statue. The people and places were vivid and full of life. They were not ideas or abstractions of reality. They *were* reality.

There are other ways of creating this reality—painting, poetry, dance, scientific and technological intuitions. Experiencing this reality within your mind, at once transcends and enfolds abstract thinking into a new kind of reality. Abstract thinking and inclusive reality are incompatible in the abstract world. They can only be fused within the mind.

The Moslems at one time acknowledged that Moslems, Jews, and Christians were "the people of the book." The Moslem book was the Koran. It conveyed abstract information from God/Allah to the world. And that is the way readers received it.

The Moslems were adept in Greek abstract thinking long before the Western world developed it. In fact, they brought abstract thinking to the West. It was vital to scientific and industrial thinking in the growth of modernity. We owe them for that.

Now we have something to give them. It comes from the reality of our art. The Koran forbids the artistic expression of the reality of life. I imagine that was to keep primitive pagan art from infecting the pure Moslem religion. Unfortunately it also short-circuited the Moslem ability to deal with the changing, flowing reality of life. But Moslems are perfectly capable of learning this new kind of artistic reality. In the novel, it is just the ability to cooperate with the author to create a new reality that depends on both. To read the Koran that way would be a blasphemy, I assume. But one could choose to read other kinds of books and participate in a new reality. Or one could choose to see three-dimensional art without encouraging paganism.

This inclusive reality of mind appears to mark the farthest evolution of the human species. If this is so, then its interior reality both supersedes and informs abstract thinking. This dimension of reality cannot exist in terms of the abstract world, but only in the inclusive spaces of the mind. In a sense, we think in modern reality, then in Islamic abstraction. We can work together, and both modernity and Islam can grow from the union.

Chapter 28

Mohammed and the Mountain

Linguistic knowing is a linear tool of thought that abstracts living and holds it static. It is dependent upon the order in which you place your words. For instance, "Mohammed came to the mountain" or "The mountain came to Mohammed" have the same words in the sentence but opposite meanings. They are rational statements—cause and effect. This is the problem Islam has in developing its thinking. Although Moslems can learn to think as moderns do (thinking in reality before abstract thinking), the only thinking they have experienced is abstract thinking. They must learn that the practical ground of reality should come before abstract thinking.

What does it take to experience this knowing of reality? You and I do it naturally; it is modern thinking. We use it without paying attention to it. It doesn't make any difference what order the words are in. We are living in a real world.

Imagine a reality of knowing that is always present inside you. For instance, imagine a shade of color that you can't see or a tone of music that you can't hear. Imagine a fragrance that you can't smell or love without flesh. Imagine a mental function that is not an idea. Those feeling tones are inner realities.

Try the following experiment on yourself. Imagine three coins lying on a table. You didn't have to count them, you *just knew* there were three. That was realistic thinking. Now imagine four coins on a table; your knowing them is probably the same kind of knowing. Now imagine five coins on a table.

Perhaps you still *just know* there are five coins. However, you may know the five coins because you analyzed them by reducing them into two categories, three and two. This reduction was the operation of an abstract mind, different from the one that *just knew*. The *just knowing* is absolute; you either know or you don't. That is reality. The knowledge arrived at by reduction is analytical and relative. The rational mind separates the coins from each other by reducing them to abstract categories.

Perhaps at five coins you still *just knew*. Go on to six or seven. Seven is usually the maximum number which can be absolutely known as direct, bound revelation. Some people have gone to nine coins, which seems to be a limit. Whatever your limit is, you can experience the difference when the abstract mind takes over.

A client of mine was trying to tune up his thinking using this procedure. I could tell he thought it was too simple an approach.

"Try it again," I told him. "Open yourself first to experience the reality of your life without abstraction. Then tell me what you *see*." I scattered five coins on the table.

He said, "Oh, what I *see*. Brown wood of the table, coins—No! quarters. Okay, now I *see* a pattern. There are five quarters lying on the brown tabletop. I didn't abstract.

"Hmm! The pattern of the quarters is obvious—the number is trivial. That makes me feel glad to be alive. I'm energized. I can feel more, feel rhythms and patterns, another kind of music. For the first time I'm in the reality of my life."

He had begun to see realistic thinking not as a technique but as a way of life opening him up and giving new meaning to reason.

I told him. "This is excellent. You are feeling the reality of thinking. It's the real world isn't it? Always available to you. Now hold onto that reality and abstract your experience in rational words. *Look* at the coins and tell me the number."

"I'm *looking* at the coins, separating them—one, two, three, four, five. But that doesn't mean anything. Reality was a rich, meaningful experience. And I also know the word, five, for what it is—a way of naming anything, not just quarters. So it's a useful way to check on reality."

Abstract thought represses the inclusive reality of thought. For example, when we shut someone's feelings out of our hearts, we feel unsettled. So what do we do? We rationalize the feeling by convincing ourselves that our lack of compassion was logically justified, thus pushing the feeling down until we don't have to be aware of an inclusive reality of thought.

Although abstraction represses inner feelings, inner feelings do not repress abstraction. In fact, an intimate life of reality is the fertile ground from which rational thought can grow. You can live securely when your inclusive reality is guiding abstract thought.

In the history of Islamic thought, no evil has gone unrationalized. With each rationalization the person becomes a little more separated from himself. Eventually, a man's true self becomes so lost that hating himself is the only way he can know that he is alive.

In our war against hatred, our ability to help Islam fight its terrorists depends on our realistic thinking. Perhaps you've known it through modern song and story—times when your eyes turned inward, dream eyes floating on currents of ethereal resonances. That is how we breathe reality into ourselves. Then we can breathe abstract linguistic thought out of that inclusive reality. Try it. Can you tell the difference? Pass it on. Feel trust in your life and discover that you are much bigger and older than you had thought. For your life's sake, learn to tune the interaction between this ancient and inclusive reality and your rational thinking.

Feeling tones you never knew you had before, wild-rushing, tingling ever-changing—all the colors and the sounds,
giving and taking, your heart full.

Chapter 29

Abstraction

We think rationally today, so we assume that is the kind of thinking the first humans had. We all know what reason is. Reason tells us that events do not occur randomly. An event causes an effect. Reason provides a way of solving problems.

But abstract, cause-and-effect reason evolved only three thousand years ago, not thirty thousand years ago. How can we know that reason is such a recent development of thinking? Let's examine some older civilizations. Four thousand years ago, the Egyptians knew that the square of the hypotenuse of a right triangle was equal to the sum of the squares of the two other sides. They could even calculate three-dimensional volumes, but they hadn't developed reason. T. E. Peet, writing on the Rhinal Mathematical Papyrus, shows how their thinking of recurring events "was never predicted on any other evidence than the fact that it had happened before on the same date or in the same circumstances. In other words, regularity had been observed but causation, even if suspected, hadn't been investigated."

Causation had not been examined in Egyptian thinking four thousand years ago, and Egyptian thinking was the leading thinking at that time. Yet in the next thousand years reason did appear. We can speculate that abstract reason began to develop soon after in Sumeria and finally bloomed in Greece in 600 A.D. The Greek philosopher and mathematician, Pythagoras, thought as abstractly as we do today. He could doubtless have followed modern mathematical theory. Since his day, abstract reason has driven the great progress of the modern world. It seems to have been as great a mental explosion as the five thousand years that marked humanity's birth.

Abstraction seeks to establish causation. Events must make *sense* or we are uncomfortable. It is as uniquely different as the realistic way of thinking. Through rational thinking information can be communicated in a linear fashion in ever more accurate detail. But what it conveys is not real life, rather it is a dissection of life, like memorizing the names of the characters in *Julius Caesar*. Reason may be smart. But is it wise?

Abstract reason may be the last evolutionary leap, but isn't it clear that reason is not enough? We need realistic thinking to ground us in the everyday world before we use the heedless abstraction of reason. All areas of human enterprise today—environment, ethnicity, war, terrorism, seem to lack this ancient wisdom. We see only disaster. We know deep in our hearts that reason unchecked could destroy the human race, just as it has the Moslem culture by giving only one set of rules to follow. We can help the Moslem world by giving it different realities. And it can help us by giving us a deeper sense of faith.

While Judaism, Christianity, and Islam all share the same cultural root, the birth of Islam around 600 A.D. represented a dramatic cultural shift. Mohammed picked up Greek abstract thinking at about the same time that Western thought lost it. Mohammed put together a one-man religion with one bible (the Koran), with one author (God speaking through Mohammed). It was cause-and-effect thinking, and it was consistent and simple. It defined civil government as well as religious faith for everyone, rich and poor, twenty-four hours a day. This was its power and its weakness. And 1400 years later, its culture has not changed.

In contrast, modern thought rediscovered abstract thinking, experiencing the Reformation and many different versions of Christianity, and developed science and technology to levels undreamed of by Moslem thinkers at their most prolific time (1000 to 1400 A.D.). The modern mind is communicated through many different religious faiths, many different languages, and many different kinds of government. That modern mind spread inclusive reality among Moslem populations. Tuning realistic thinking, especially in terms of art and literature, is something anyone can learn. However, to fanatical Moslems, these inner ways of thinking seemed to be a deadly infection to their religion rather than a salvation. The revolution which I encountered in Pakistan twenty-five years ago was their response to this infection.

It didn't have to be that way. I think of that magic time in Seville from 1100 to 1300 when Islam and Western thinking were each giving the best of their philosophy and literature and science during a time of freedom of thought.

Certainly it was here that Western mind reclaimed the forgotten cause and effect of Greek thinking. That *intention* is what remains. And our intentions are themselves encompassed—enfolded—by mind. If we pay attention, we can see that the human mind includes every fallen sparrow, every hair that turns white. In our time-enfolded, mind-enfolded universe, nothing and no one is ever lost.

You can break through the boundaries of past-present-future. In fact, you do it all the time. You have an inner sense of growing older, of changing in all kinds of ways. You can sense that you are everything you have ever been. The reality of your flow of change has never been interrupted to create an abstract *now*.

Chapter 30

The Modern Way to Think

By uncovering the cultural roots of humanity, you can encounter the continuity of inclusive reality out of which you yourself have grown. You can be part of an unceasing flow of presences that have been passed on for thousands of years and hundreds of lives to you.

Knowing reality is like dancing—it is alive with rhythm and movement. You have been dancing in various ways since you were a child. Absorbing the emotional rhythms and patterns of ordinary life is how children create their minds. The spontaneous shapes and rhythms of children's dances reiterate the way we become human beings.

Let yourself dance in your mind. Discern the rhythms and feeling tones passed down to you from ancient times. Notice the feeling tones of buildings, the rhythms of columns and windows, the movements of arches. Great architecture is the gift to you of the shapes of the reality of human continuity. The meter of words in poetry gives you meaning. The art of drama communicates inclusive reality to you directly.

And music plays the shapes of human rhythms and tones. Art uses the language of holistic reality.

Carl Rogers said that science was a way to keep us from misleading ourselves. But to discover our human self, science must also use artistic mediums—rhythms, tones, and patterns.

Mental evolution brings along what it started with, just as physical evolution does. Your body includes cells that developed millions and even billions of years ago. With a few exceptions, like the appendix, every element created over our four million years of physical evolutionary history is used in our bodies today. Our lives and health depend on everything working together, just as thinking requires that we work with all three modes in balance. It is the natural way of thinking.

The trouble is that we assume abstraction is the ultimate way of thinking in our mental evolutionary process, so we can forget the other two. But that doesn't work in mental evolution any more than in physical evolution. In particular, we need practical reality along with rational thinking. That is the natural order. Each time we think rationally, we need holistic wondering to precede it as a guide to the reality of life. That is being wise.

How do we find this realistic thinking? It is present below all our rational thinking, but it remains unacknowledged. We simply have to pay attention to it.

The importance of the inclusive reality of modern thought is not what it enables modern people to do. Rather, it is what it renders them incapable of doing—things like terrorism, exclusion, and inhumanity.

Anyone can experience reality anywhere in the world regardless of race, sex, creed, or intelligence. It is just that in the West it appears to have reached a critical mass in the population. Critical mass means that this reality of thinking has been spreading through modernity at an ever-increasing rate, while there has been little increase throughout Islam.

Chapter 31

Creative Reality

Some of our greatest thinkers have retained a sense of inclusive reality all their lives. Albert Einstein, Martin Heidegger, and Rollo May come to mind. To meet one of these people, come with me to the little town of Princeton, New Jersey. The time is 1941. This morning Albert Einstein has left the Institute for Advanced Study and is walking down Nassau Street to pick up a prescription at the drugstore. Across the street are the wooded lawns and the old buildings of the university. He is wearing a threadbare Harris tweed overcoat over baggy flannel pants. A long, gray, wool scarf is wrapped around his neck and hangs almost to the ground. He comes to a sun-filled recess in the worn, orange brick wall of the drugstore and stops for a minute out of the wind. As he looks around at the trees, his innocent eyes are filled with wonder. Whatever he sees fills him with wonder. He notices me in wonder. I venture a question, "Could you explain the universe inside of me the way you have explained the universe outside me?"

He leans back against the wall regarding me for a moment, then for another moment, in wonder. Finally he says in his soft voice, "I can describe the outside universe in an equation—in the abstract. But the universe that is in you—that is where I live, too. I can only approach that with reverence. It is through that inner universe that I discover things about the outside universe that guide me in my mathematics. We call it Gedanska in Germany."

Gedanska is a word describing a quality of thought that most truly great scientists such as Einstein and Newton possessed. It is not rational thought because reason is only one-dimensional, working in a straight line from a cause to an effect. Gedanska implies an inner realistic way of thinking that grasps the bigger picture. One wonders, "What if . . . ?" When those inner realistic wonderings form a definite shape, the tool of reason is applied to designate an effect—a solution, practical and easily communicated. With Einstein, realistic thinking was so implicit in all his thoughts that he paused for that extra moment of wonder in an inconsequential exchange with a student before expressing himself. But it has stayed with me all my life—that moment of wisdom not fully appreciated for many years.

Einstein's greatest discoveries came from following inclusive realities and then expressing them rationally. He wondered about riding a beam of light while looking back at a static clock tower. Then he took the experience of his reality and applied abstract thinking, developing the theory of special relativity. He wondered about being in a falling elevator so that he was weightless. He experienced this feeling over and over, living in the way of practical reality until he could reproduce all its different aspects and continuities. When he finished, he arrived at the mathematical equation of the theory of general relativity—that gravity and acceleration are the same. This is the way all of us should tune up our thinking. It works for every aspect of daily life.

Martin Heidegger was different. He was a thinker about the problems of thinking. He said, "Reason is the most stiff-necked adversary of thought."

You may say, "But I have spent sixteen years of my life in school learning to think in the abstract. They didn't even have a name for this other realistic way of thinking."

That was exactly what Heidegger meant by stiff-necked. Reason was inflexible and short-sighted, it needed a realistic guide, but training in abstractions actively excluded such a nonreasonable guide. On the other hand, if the three-dimensional guide was present, reason could use its own stiff-necked discipline of thought to express it in practical terms. Think about when you were in high school. Your literature teacher assigned a play to read, say Shakespeare's *Julius Caesar*. Possibly you fanned through the book, picking up names and sequences of action. In half an hour you were through and could get on with your other homework. That was the smart thing to do. On the other hand, you might have actually read it, thrilled by its dramatic passion. From the point of view of getting top grades, that was a dumb thing to do. We intuitively understand that regardless of what the school says, it is there to teach us reason. But *Julius Caesar* is art—inclusive reality. If we are interested in doing well in life, we opt for the simplest way to the top grades. It may not be wise, but it is smart.

Teachers also understand that their job is to teach rational thinking. In fact, as Heidegger realized, teachers may not be aware of any other kind of thinking. If you are interested in the ancient wonder of realistic thinking, some in school may believe you are fleeing to the past. There is a sense that the cultural past is unhealthy. Of course you cannot get to the future without the past. Einstein would have told you that there is no present—go directly from the past to the future.

Making good grades in school is a predictor of success in life. However, this is a very recent phenomenon. I can remember only fifty years ago when a survey was made of the school grades of the presidents of the country's largest corporations. They averaged out with a C. Learning to reason well in school was not, at that time, a predictor of success. It was important, but there were holistic, experiential ways of thinking that were also important.

Unfortunately even holistic wonder can be rationalized today. Moslems are experts at doing this. As you feel a moment of wonder, your mind, educated to reason, will present rational reasons for this wonder, dismissing your realistic thinking. Eventually your thinking can become a series of rationalizations, so that only hypocrisy is left. The problem is that these two ways of thinking are so different, they cannot exist at the same time and place. One is inclusive, realistic thought, and the other is an abstraction expressed in a one-dimensional way. Rationalizations may not be *right*, but they are *reasonable*. There are always reasonable ways to explain what you do or think even when they are *not* right. You have to *get it right* by putting your realistic thinking first. Then use rational words as tools to explain it. Another Nobel laureate, F. A. Hayek once said, "It may indeed prove to be far the most difficult and not the least important task for human reason . . . to comprehend its own limitations."

Another creative thinker, Rollo May, was a wondering psychologist. He regarded each person who came to him with overwhelming wonder at their reality. Only after realistic thought would his rational thinking be engaged. Rollo May regarded each person as a continuity of life from the birth of humanity. While Einstein wondered at the continuity of the universe, May wondered at the continuity of individual souls. His goal was to find the right tone, rhythm, word, that this particular person could vibrate with, that would open him up to the continuity of his ancient realistic mind. Rollo May was my closest friend and mentor. It was while working with him that I stumbled upon a disquieting observation: People believe that they rationally choose a course of action.

To illustrate this, let me tell you about a client. Her name is Betty, and she is heading for a shock. We have been talking about the tuning of realistic thinking in her life.

She has been touched by a faint awareness of the limits of her rational thinking. Her brilliance of mind has been overfocused on the surface of thought—reason manipulating words. But everything about her—the way she sits in alignment with gravity, the fluidity of her hand as she pushes back a heavy mass of dark hair—in the quiet room all these shout of an evanescent power of modern thought she doesn't know she has.

I suggest that we could try to understand the discrepancy between her actions and her rational decisions to act.

She looks up at me sharply, "Discrepancy? What discrepancy?" She is shocked. "I came here to improve my thinking. Let's get with it."

Her sense of reality is shaken when she discovers that she does not, in fact, do what she had decided to do, even when thinking in the abstract. She may decide to take a particular action, but then she actually does something else. Rationally she decides to give up drinking, but she doesn't give it up. Where is her free will, her freedom of choice? Her life is turned upside down. But what if there is a cultural will greater than her rational will—a will of hardly noticed vibrations, rhythms, and patterns of thought? They are her realistic thinking.

Some people think naturally with all of their different ways of thinking tuned up. They aren't surprised at the suggestion that deliberate rational choice doesn't guide their actions. They are already aware that modern thinking is the major guide to what they do.

Betty once said, "I'm not aware of any other forces guiding what I do, so it doesn't happen." But of course she was not aware of other guiding forces because she had been trained not to pay attention to them. But now Betty is aware of that censorship of thought and finds that allowing her modern realistic thinking to guide her rational choices brings a dimension of power into her life she had never imagined.

A NEW WORLD

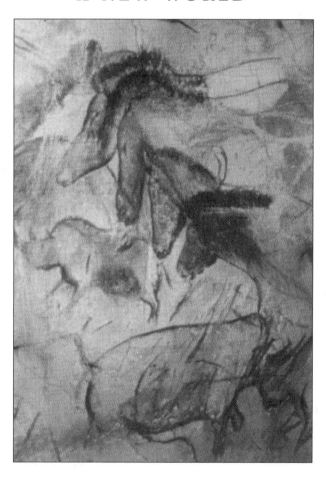

VIII

WHAT WE CAN DO

CHAPTER 32

Were You Ever a Terrorist?

Each one of us knows anger, hatred, self-pity, humiliation, helplessness, or impotence. So, to some extent, each of us knows the terrorist mind through our own experience.

In the sixties I was staying with Tom Wolfe at his house in San Francisco. He was working on his book, *The Right Stuff*. We were both trying to understand the minds of the flower children cropping up in San Francisco from all over the country. Haight-Ashbury became the center of the communes, the free love, the freedom from possessions, the drugs. The Hog Farm was the name of a young commune group that entertained us. Ken Keasey and his Marry Pranksters were getting ready to tour the country's universities. And every morning the streets turned up another child's body.

I have a dream about those years. I see a sunlit field with spring's first wildflowers. The field is tilted steeply upward. It is covered with young people striving to reach the top, which glistens with their hopes of a spiritual life. Then, about midway up, they pause and start to party. Drugs flow. A few press on, but their friends call them back, "Come talk about peace and love." No one reaches the top.

Caught in the middle with nowhere to go, groups of flower children sometimes became terrorists. The Weathermen set off bombs and robbed banks. Some of these groups, like the Symbionese Liberation Army, reached the depths by kidnapping innocent people like Patty Hearst. For them, the peace sign signalled war, and love became hate. Do you see a difference between these young American terrorists from good families and the terrorists of the Islamic Movement? I don't. It is interesting to note that, just as the Islamic terrorists make slaves of their women, this was also a tendency followed by the men of our homegrown flower-children-turned-terrorists. Among us right now are terrorist groups like the New Ecologists. We must quell their acts of violence just as vigorously as those of Al-Qaida. The United States must be the example of a terrorist-free country.

Depending on your generation, you might have flirted with terrorism or known someone, who, unable to reach a higher goal, settled into hate and self-pity. I knew some of the flower children, I counseled some. Of course most of them became good citizens and good people—benefitting from their experience.

Some years later I went to Guatemala City to meet with officials about their young terrorists. As I was about to step off the curb, my government bodyguard stopped me. He said, "You're about to step into the blood stains of your United States ambassador who was assassinated here."

My appointment with the Guatemalan Cabinet was at night. I was in an armored car in the middle of a caravan of three vehicles. There were flashes of gun fire. We were driving along a residential street with beautiful homes. In our headlights I could see soldiers surrounding one of the houses. We finally came to a block of low buildings, passing three rings of surveillance before getting to a nondescript structure. Once inside, we passed more rings of surveillance. When I reached the men I was to see, one of them said, "We move frequently. If they knew where we were, they would blow us up. These terrorists are all young people from our best families." The government was fighting the terrorists from house to house throughout the city.

The next day I was meeting with some bankers when one man said to his friend, "Jorge, I heard the government killed your son last night, I'm sorry." I felt a surge of guilt shoot through me. I had been out on those streets last night.

I knew I must have looked odd because Jorge, a heavy-set man, turned to me and said, "My son would have killed me if he could. How can I be sorry that he's dead. He has to be dead if we are to save the country." But Jorge's eyes were blank, his heavy flesh weighing him down.

On my way back to the United States, I remember thinking that Guatemala was in an impossible situation. Everyone had become dehumanized. That seemed unthinkable. Could it happen in the United States?

It didn't, but it could have.

Still, terror is alive and well in the United States. Look at the attacks on abortion clinics. These are not really about whether abortions are moral or immoral. They are about hatred and obsession. They are about terrorists doing something to hurt someone else. How can obsession or hatred determine what is right? We know what it takes to know what is right. It takes realistic thinking.

Chapter 33

Freedom Fighters or Terrorists?

Reuter's, the British wire service, won't use the term "terrorist" because the reader might confuse *freedom fighter* with *terrorist*. In Islam and the United States there should be no confusion. If the freedom fighter is organized to violently hurt civilians, he is a terrorist. He can act by himself and still be motivated by the terrorist mind. An Islamic or United States terrorist may describe himself as a freedom fighter. And, although you may not be able to define all terrorist acts, you know them when you see them.

Some say that the United States is so powerful, so rich and pampered, that we *cause* terrorists to hate us and kill us. Do you feel pampered and rich? I don't. Do you think you have *caused* terrorists to hate you? I don't think so. The reason terrorists hate us is because that is the way they think.

Actually, the food aid organizations, the human rights groups, and the professors of Middle East studies who live in this country have, over the last fifty years, encouraged the terrorists to think that you owe them something. We have spent billions of dollars and countless hours in the service of the poor and the oppressed of the world. When we started these programs, would-be terrorists didn't hate us. Now they do. They have learned that hatred pays. Does that make you feel good, that you have been literally programming terrorists to kill you?

Yes, we need people with open hearts to act for us to feed the hungry of the world. But we must realize that when we give material help to the unfortunate, we also affect the way they think. Do we know how those who act for us think about our country? Can open hearts bring an open mind to the world? I pray they can. Their actions can do much good in the world. And they can be on the front line in waging the war on the terrorist mind.

Victim, pity, humiliation, impotence, contempt, are words human rights groups use to describe terrorists. But U.S. psychotherapists have adopted another word used by human rights groups—self-esteem. They claim that low self-esteem *causes* people to feel worthless and perform terrorist acts.

However, current research indicates that artificially increasing anyone's self-esteem, including terrorists, does not change their thinking or their behavior. In fact, it encourages the way they have been thinking.

Freud long ago said that he strove to help his patients achieve meaningful work and meaningful love. He never said lack of self-esteem caused anything. Feeling worthless is just feeling worthless. If you are not rewarded for being worthless you might do something worthwhile. Maybe the terrorists should change the way they think.

Abstract thinking idealizes Islamics as poor, innocent people oppressed by evil capitalistic societies. It envisions the future as a socialistic society in which capitalistic evil is redeemed and everyone lives in peace.

The trouble is that concrete reality has not guided this abstract expression of human life. Some intellectuals find the practical reality of life so messy and unpredictable that it is more comfortable for them to think in abstractions.

It may also be that abstract reason, having to give up the inconsistencies of religion, has found a more pleasant refuge in social studies, which are consistent and easy to believe in. It feels especially at home in the Moslem religion, finding the rules of the Koran more consistent than the dogma of other religions and, in the abstract, more comfortable.

The New York Times recently referred to members of the 1960s' U.S. Symbionese Liberation Army as *radicals*. The dictionary defines "radical" as "favoring thorough-going but constitutional reform." Those young people had no constitutional plans to make things better. They were violent terrorists. Gandhi and Martin Luther King were nonviolent agents of change; they were not terrorists.

Freedom fighters violently fight and kill people. If we want to wage war on terrorists-cum-freedom-fighters, we must know who they are. That means we must have a practical reality of terrorism that applies to everyone equally. Islamic terrorists are not fighting for *freedom*; they are fighting to take away modern freedoms to establish an Islamic state with very few freedoms—especially for women.

Also, they are no longer fighting within a *particular* country. They are fighting to establish a Moslem *world*. In Southeast Asia, Jemaah Islamia pledged to establish Doulah-Islamiah, a country combining Malaysia, Singapore, Indonesia, and the Philippines. "Freedom fighters" are tied to international terror.

Recently, an Islamic council defined terrorism. Or perhaps it would be more accurate to say that it *undefined* terrorism. In the council's words, nothing, it seems, is terrorism—not even the suicide bombings by Palestinians against Israeli citizens.

I think the average American citizen knows the reality that terror-ists want to kill him. As a result, we now want to know all about terrorists. Where they come from. How they are different from us. How they think—especially how they think. We need to understand the terrorist mind.

We know that terrorists are afraid to declare war. They just want to kill in the abstract until someone gives up. The people they kill are not human to them. And they have no rights. I will repeat my short definition: Terrorists express self-hate through organized violence. So human rights groups can define terrorism if they really want to.

But what about human rights? I think people are uncertain about defining a human rights organization. I know I am. Isn't every "right" human? It's made by humans. Isn't a *right* whatever the people who run the human rights organizations say that it is? I don't think these people necessarily represent the American understanding of terrorism. They think in abstractions. They sometimes seem to be helping the terrorists in foreign countries. They believe America is guilty and responsible for the ills of the world.

The United Nations does not define terrorism. The Secretary General, Kofi Anaan, said, "We should all be clear that there is no trade-off between effective action against terrorism and the protection of human rights." In other words, you're not allowed to fight terror-ism by infringing on human rights. But what are human rights? Laws enacted by our Congress? I don't think that is what Kofi Anaan has in mind.

In World War II we fire-bombed the citizens of Dresden and other towns in Germany. I don't believe that Kofi Anaan would include bombing citizens as a human right. If he had been a powerful inter-national figure then, Hitler might have won. Also, Anaan believes the Palestinians are freedom fighters waging a just war. Doesn't he realize that Hitler's Holocaust did not end in Europe, but is still going on even more bitterly in Palestine today?

Arafat said, "I want to negotiate peace as long as it doesn't humiliate Palestinians"—which means, Palestinians will be humiliated until all Israelis are dead. Then we will have peace.

Who gets to decide what is a right? The United Nations has a Declaration of Human Rights. Who got to decide that? Amnesty International ran an article recently in *The New York Times* saying that the human rights of the prisoners in Guantanamo Bay were violated because some were hooded and shackled or sedated during the plane ride over. Who got to decide those rights?

The Declaration of Independence says government through consent of the governed shall establish laws to protect the unalienable rights of men born equal. These *rights* are life, liberty, and the pursuit of happiness.

A Moslem government took control of Sudan, with its capitol in Khartoum. The south part of Sudan is inhabited by primitive animist Christians. The Moslem government attempts to enforce Sharias law in the Christian South. Sharias law is from the Koran. Women (not men—who are unfaithful) are stoned to death for infidelity.

The Christians are starving, so the United Nations buys grain from the Moslem government in the North and flies the grain to the South. The Moslem North then takes the United Nations money and buys arms to capture slaves in the South. This is the biggest slave trade in the world today.

Some say the UN inadvertently finances the slave trade here. But Arabs were the largest slave traders back in the 1700s. The trade died down but now has increased again. You can see long lines of men and women chained together trudging across the dry, sandy soil of Sudan. The guards terrorize them. In fact, the guards do anything they please with the slaves.

I worked in Nigeria, South and West of Sudan, for a time, counseling on a liquid gas plant. There was again a more or less comfortable mix of Christians and Moslems. Recently, however, a Nigerian Moslem government has been trying to impose Sharias law among the Christians. This does not mean the people have more freedom. They have less freedom.

Human Rights Watch reported that all the Afghan war had accomplished was a return of oppression, and that the civilian casualties may constitute violations of international humanitarian law. What kind of an international law is that?

Some people get angry at the plight of poor, hungry people around the world. That gives them an emotional high. It's a high that exalts them personally. When the high diminishes, all they have to do is think in the abstract about those suffering people and the emotional high returns. Over the years the anger turns to hate toward those who don't agree with them. Then finally the hate becomes self-hate. Even though they think with the perspectives of modernity, they become unable to see the reality of what they do. They even show hate for those who imprison Al-Qaida fighters at Guantanamo Bay. But the reality is that those imprisoned terrorists may know of another attack on our country which will kill your family and mine.

Some say that the single-minded devotion to human rights in the world leads to a kind of arrogance which assumes that abstract values are the best for everyone. But everyone doesn't have to think the way human rights activists do. I suggest that human rights are a legacy of the flower children.

I know and admire many of those in human rights organizations. Their hearts are big, and they are sincere in their concern for the downtrodden. That used to be admirable, didn't it? Yes, and it still is. But there is now a more important issue—self-survival.

The Moslem culture is ancient and proud. Our culture is different. But we *can* work together. Each of us has something valuable to offer the other. We can grow together through cooperation.

Chapter 34

Dealing with Hatred Daily

Consider a man who cannot control his wife and children. For him control defines who he is. He is nothing without control. He hates his family. He hates himself. He is obsessed. So he kills his wife and children. Then he kills himself. That is his final claim to identity. Is he a terrorist? I think so. He is punished for such an act in the United States. An Islamic terrorist might kill his wife out of self-hatred. And if he had believed his wife was not chaste, he would have little trouble having her stoned to death. The need and ability to control one's wife is not considered a pathology and crime in the Moslem world as it is in the United States; there it is considered a man's right.

We have a law in the United States about hate crimes. Anyone committing a crime out of hate is given a more severe sentence. If you drive a car when you are in a fit of rage and you have an accident, that could be considered a hate crime. It is like driving when you are intoxicated. This kind of law could be a help in controlling terrorist tendencies in the United States. It underscores how your mind and your thoughts are important in this war on terrorism.

Everyone feels hatred for someone else from time to time. But that emotion will last for about three minutes and then die away. But if the person abstracts the event, perhaps thinking, "That guy doesn't think I'm important enough to listen to me," then the emotion reappears. Each time he rationalizes to recharge his hatred, he gets a little high, a little pumped up, until hatred becomes an obsessive addiction. Soon it becomes self-hatred.

If that happens to you, you are doing what terrorists do. That kind of thinking shapes the terrorist mind.

I know that I am capable of hate. I can imagine how people can grow up in a society where hate boils every minute of every day. If they're young it only takes a few years to take its toll. We see it in cults that brainwash our children, or in some man in a city who comes home and kills his wife and children and then himself. The possibility of self-hate exists everywhere in the world and in the recesses of our own hearts.

Remember at the beginning I wrote about hate being one of the signs of a terrorist mind? I wrote about my client Miriam, and how to avoid turning hate into self-hate by experimenting with balancing reality with abstraction by practicing the hate exercise. I practice it myself. My routine takes about five minutes. I experience all the emotion of hate. I feel it first in my stomach as a hot flame; then it moves up to my chest. I am taking deep breaths, my pulse rises, I feel warm as my blood flow increases. Then my hatred travels up my neck and out the top of my head.

There is nothing or no one to rationalize or blame, so my abstract rational thinking doesn't kick in and my holistic thinking of what is real accepts it for what it is—a healthy, cleansing emotion. After the hatred builds up, the energized emotion takes about three minutes to go away.

If we can learn this exercise ourselves, and if the Islamic people can learn it, self-hate will turn into self-respect.

Chapter 35

Iraqi Oil, United States Oil

Iraq is a special case in the Mideast. Oil is the key. Iraq could be producing six million barrels of oil every day. At present, because of United Nations restrictions enforced by the United States and England, it produces only a trickle. Iraq, in full production, might produce more than Saudi Arabia. Let's be clear; the Iraqis surrendered unconditionally to the allied forces. They do not decide the restrictions imposed on them, the allies do. Yet Saddam continues to try to bargain. Clearly, in his mind, Iraq did not surrender unconditionally. The war is still going on for him. All he needs to do is stop the war and open up Iraq. Then he could produce the oil.

It is perfectly well understood by the Saudis that their position in the oil market is at stake. Imagine Saddam Hussein saying privately to the Saudis, "We're on the same underlying oil field. If I am defeated, I guarantee that I have the dirty bombs to take out your oil production. You keep the United States off of us or you will suffer too." That, of course, is a wild supposition, but it could happen. Then the world supply of oil could suffer a crisis. The European nations get 70 percent of their oil from Saudi Arabia. They are naturally concerned with a stable oil market.

On the other hand, if Iraq is conquered, it could supply lost Saudi oil; the crisis would be ameliorated. The country that takes Saddam out will eventually control the oil market. The United States will not have a problem getting partners in the war. The partners will all have a say in the development of Iraqi oil. Russia is also a player in the Mideast oil situation. It will soon have completed its oil pipeline to the Mediterranean and would do most anything to block the development of competing Iraqi oil.

But whatever happens in the international oil market, the United States must be free of dependence domestically on the Mideast oil. We only get 10 percent of our oil from the Saudis, but we can't fight Iraq if we depend on anyone in the Mideast for oil. The Saudis probably wouldn't cut off their oil, but it would be a great time to blackmail us again.

Here are some ways we can conserve oil.

Drive using natural gas. Buses in British Columbia use natural gas. Boone Pickens sells natural gas at filling stations in Arizona. In Texas 25,000 cars are fueled by natural gas. These people are doing the right thing without government action. Any truck that uses diesel fuel could use natural gas instantly. Use a compressed natural gas tank instead of the gasoline tank. Any car running on gasoline could be adapted easily to use natural gas. Natural gas is a nonpolluting fuel. It produces 70 percent less smog than gasoline and 96 percent less toxins and carcinogens from gasoline. This is an example of a simple change that could reduce our oil consumption drastically.

In the war on terrorism we can't wait twenty years to develop hydrogen-fueled motors. Anyone could change to natural gas right now. It would not take a law. And it might become the policy of other countries. Cutting oil sales in the Islamic world could reduce the money now used to finance terrorist schools, especially since the pipeline from Russia to the Mediterranean will be shortly completed. Russia is the biggest producer of oil at the present time, and will become a powerful competitor with Middle Eastern oil when their pipeline reaches Mediterranean ports.

But guess what? As I am writing this, the Environmental Protection Agency has banned conversion to natural gas over the entire country. Their *stated concern* is that they don't have the ability to control the conversions to natural gas. You don't think their *concern* might be the goodwill of the gasoline refineries? They are the ones paying the Saudis all that money that finances world terrorism.

I have never bought the idea that drilling for oil damaged the environment, although the use of oil certainly damages the environment more than any other energy source. Drilling wells would cut down our overseas purchases.

Anyone who drives can choose to curtail excessive use of his or her car. In some cases, people can car-pool or come up with other creative or cooperative ways to get around. As a consumer, I can choose not to purchase a gas-hungry automobile. If cutting our gasoline consumption would deny the Saudis some of the billions of dollars that fund terrorists all over the world, that seems very worthwhile.

Another way to cut down on our oil consumption would be to set our thermostats on 68 degrees in the winter. This is an individual action. We don't have to wait for the president to ask.

I'm sure we are technology-wise and resourceful enough to come up with other options. If you have discovered some useful ways to reduce oil consumption, I'd like to hear about them.

Chapter 36

Leading by Example

The United States seems to have developed a method of fighting that brings the infantry, the air force, and the navy into minute-by-minute coordination. This may give the United States a military advantage that will last for some years—much like the massed archery King Henry V used against the French at Agincourt. But it is a temporary advantage.

If we are going to uproot terrorism in our world, now is the time to do it. So where do we begin?

First, we have to define what modern people can agree on as being terror. I will repeat my short definition: Self-hate expressed through organized violence. A longer version might be: Terrorism is the organized indiscriminate, arbitrary, unpredictable, coercive use of violence that is motivated by hatred, lack of trust, and a refusal to see the reality of the world it lives in.

Second, military action is a necessity, but it will not and cannot cleanse the world of terrorism. Only education will rid people of self-hatred and instill in them the ability to trust others and understand inclusive reality.

Third, as Americans we need to present ourselves as a model to the world. We are the most diverse nation on the planet. One of the most hopeful signs I noticed in our country after the September eleventh attack was the uniformity of our reaction. Americans of many nationalities felt "terrorists have done this to me, to my country. We are all together in this effort." Even minorities, often raised to be victims and to be humiliated by discrimination, felt this solidarity.

We must hold and treasure that belief. In one strong voice Americans must continue to say, "Our country includes all of us." And we must all be sure that it is true. That means we must work to eradicate the self-defeating mind of terrorism. We must not feel we are victims. We may be hurt by life, but we don't have to be victims. And we can certainly choose to rise above self-pity.

If you go to a psychological group session on addiction, you will find people being asked what they hate: "Don't you hate your addiction? You can't live with it and you can't live without it. The addiction is a high you can't do without." The next question is "Why do you hate yourself?"

If terrorists came to a group session, the question would be the same: "Why do you hate yourself?" A true answer would be, "I'm addicted to the incredible emotional high it gives me. . . . It makes me feel strong and alive."

If we ever hope to cure this addiction, we must know what terrorism is and keep our own self-hate under control. Here are some things that we can do for ourselves and to set an example for the world:

- Recall what Supreme Court Judge Jackson said, "The Constitution of the United States is not a suicide pact." There is no right to destroy this country.

- Include personal diversity and personal change. Inclusiveness is strong. Know whom to trust.
- Recognize that inclusion does not mean tolerance.
- Tolerance does not have a right and wrong. Anything may be tolerated, even if it will destroy us. Tolerance is weak.
- Live in reality, in tune with both practical reality and abstract thinking.
- Live in trust. Trust is knowing what is right. Rules are not very helpful in knowing right and wrong, good and evil. Rules are abstract. They are not alive.
- Sharpen two other abilities that will help you to trust. First, learn to walk in another person's shoes. Second, internalize that experience to an inclusive reality of that person.
- Remember that lack of trust is a mark of the terrorist mind.
- Recognize that Islam lives by abstract rules. They can't tell you whom to trust. Trust must refer to an individual. It is not abstract. As a result, terrorists lie to each other and to the world.
- Nourish a self that cannot be humiliated. If you know who you are, you may feel bad that someone is trying to humiliate you, but that doesn't mean you are humiliated. The only person who can humiliate you is yourself.

IX

VICTORS

Chapter 37

Middle-East Victors

In the Saudi religious schools children learn self-pity and self-hate. They nurture the terrorist mind. It only takes a few years for everyone to be thinking alike. Islam is made up of Arabic Moslem states and Moslem states of other races. There are huge differences between the Arab states and those Moslem states of other races. And even among Arabic states there are differences. In the Middle East today, Tunisia, Algeria, and Turkey have fought their own battles with terrorism and *won*. If we want to win the war on terrorism, we must pay attention.

Tunisia

Tunisia is taking back its schools from the terrorist teachers. They teach now that Islam can work in an inclusive modern world, that you don't have to hate.

In the late 1980s the Islamic Movement tried to use terror to overthrow the Tunisian government. The most effective move of the government of Zine Abidine Ben Ali was to take over the schools. School books that degraded women were destroyed. Now required courses include Freud's psychology, Darwin's evolution, The Universal Declaration of Human Rights, and the value of the individual.

In addition, the government fought terrorism with mass arrests and anti-terrorism laws. The mosques were nationalized. The doors were open only for prayers, and sermons were led by government employees.

The government then attacked pockets of poverty, bringing them electricity and water. Now the country has a prosperous middle class. Seventy-five percent of families own their own homes. Women don't wear veils and outnumber men in schools. The country is stable and is looking toward a vital future.

The only problem for Tunisia is that human rights groups like Amnesty International, academics, and journalists are there to support the rights of the freedom fighters—freedom fighters the government says are terrorists.

Algeria

A defiant enemy of terror was the Algerian novelist, Tajar Djaout. At the beginning of the terrible terrorist attack on his country he wrote, "If you speak, you die . . . If you are silent, you die . . . so speak and die."

On May 26, 1993, terrorists assassinated him. He was 39 years old. It was a brutal time. One hundred thousand people were killed before the government prevailed. The last sentence Djaout wrote was, "Will there be another spring?"

Yes. Terrorism has been defeated. The government seems steady and looks toward a prosperous future, perhaps even with close ties to the European Union.

However, human rights activists have proclaimed the terrorists to be freedom fighters, to be protected at all costs. Let us pray that their objectives do not betray this victory over terrorism.

Uzbekistan

The Moslem countries that used to belong to the Soviet Union have had similar experiences. In Uzbekistan, for example, terrorists struck at the state in 1999. Today they are dead or in jail. Membership in the terrorist organization, Hizb-ut-Tahrir, can be treated as treason. Samara Uinarova has a brother who has just been sentenced to twenty years in prison. She says that her brother will be an old man when he gets out, that he's not a terrorist, he's a believer. The government says that he is a believer and a terrorist.

The Human Rights Watch complains that Uzbekistan has an appalling human rights record. On the other hand, Feriza Insavacleov, a Moslem Uzbeki, says the government is doing the right thing. She says that soon after Uzbekistan became independent from Russia, missionaries from Saudi Arabia began pouring in and built hundreds of mosques. Her little brother Eldor was brainwashed by the new missionaries. Soon Eldor was becoming aggressive and insulting to the women in his family. Feruza feared that her brother was being lost to a cult. The family decided that Eldor be forbidden to go to the mosque, and he obeyed his family. Now he is 19 and earning a good salary at a textile mill. He has his own cell phone and agrees that many of the things the Imam told him were wrong.

Afghanistan

In the 1930s, a Pakistani named Abdul Ghaffar Khan led a pacifist movement in Northwest Afghanistan. His contemporary, Mohandas Gandhi, called this Moslem movement a miracle. Ghaffar's interpretation of Jihad was putting one's life in the hands of enemies without killing them. He wanted a secular not Islamic state. When he died at 98 (in 1988), his followers formed a caravan of peace and love to carry his body to Jalalabad in Afghanistan. Today it seems incredible that a Moslem tribe fifty years ago could have practiced peace and love.

Egypt

In the 1950s, Gamal Abdel Nasser, the president of Egypt, fought successfully against the Moslem Brotherhood for a secular state and a liberal Arab accommodation to the modern world. President Sadat, following him, made peace with Israel and was assassinated by Moslem fanatics. Under Mubarak, Sadat's successor, the terrorists responsible were wiped out, and Egypt continues as a secular country with secular schools available to the citizens, but terror is growing in spite of government efforts. It may be that the only long-term solution is an Islamic literary response to terror. Madam Mubarak was on the right track with her literary schools in the 1980s.

Bosnia

We went to war to save Bosnia from the Serbs. Bosnia had a Moslem society comfortable with the West. Now Saudi Arabia is spending millions to create a terrorist society there.

If there are a pair of villains in the spread of terrorism, they are Saudi Arabia and the United States. We give the Saudis billions for their oil, and they spend the money, even in Bosnia, for terrorism.

Bosnians, a majority of whom are Moslems, have long considered themselves the most moderate believers in the world. They are of Christian stock, converted to Islam when the Turks conquered them five hundred years ago. They survived as Moslems under fifty years of communist rule, becoming more and more comfortable with the modern mind. They drink liquor and fail to observe many other Moslem rules. But since the war in Bosnia, Saudi charitable offices have spent more than half a million dollars there to build mosques and encourage strict Moslem observance. NATO police have raided these offices to break up their terrorist threat.

Europe

In France 10 percent of the population is Moslem. In England, Northern Ireland, Sweden, Spain, and Germany about 5 percent are Moslems. These countries have sheltered some of the most dangerous cells of Moslem terrorists.

In most countries in Europe, Moslems are concentrating on the Koran as the basis of how they live personally. They say the Koran has all the rules both of civil and religious governance for one's life. The individual can follow the Koran without any help. They don't want the Islamic (cultural) practices imposed by the imams and their Madrassas. The cloak of the imams is the best cloak for power in their home countries, but not in Europe.

If Moslem modernism is to get a second chance, it should be in Europe and the United States. Nevertheless, even these most modern Moslems seem to be slipping away from Western thought. Saudi Arabia has spent hundreds of millions of dollars setting up mosques and schools preaching the terrorist mind in the West. In Germany the young sons of well-off modern Moslem parents who have lived there all their lives, say Islam cannot and will not live with democracy. They live smugly in the knowledge that their incipient terror will be protected at all costs by the modern human rights groups.

A Moslem in Europe grows up within the safety and security of the rules and penalties of the Koran. His self-image is the Koran. He cannot understand how he could live without this faith which has one absolute message to give him a common identity.

He grows up in a society with little faith compared to his. In modernity each person must create an inclusive realistic self. He struggles to keep Islam and modernity tuned. They each have a place to play in his life. This is the ideal situation. He can grow up to be a healthy Islamic person in a modern culture. There are many Moslems like him.

Or he may live continually hating, a victim humiliated by the modern mind. He usually falls into self-hate. He can refuse to accept that he is living in an inclusive culture. This is the worst condition, and he is lost to self-hate. Then he finds a Saudi-financed mosque with a fanatical teacher, and sooner or later he is introduced to a terrorist cell.

It seems clear that even in Europe and the United States an inclusive mind is not enough.

Turkey's Breakthrough

We've been following the adventures of Islam and modern culture during the last twenty-five years of domination by the Saudi conservative Moslem religion. A general observation is that the growth of Wahhabism brings terror. Some countries such as Liberia and Algeria have faced their terror. The terrorists have been killed, the terrorist mind debunked, and more individual freedom has been extended to the population. It has been a bitter fight for these Islamic countries, but they have done better than modernity in terms of terrorism.

Turkey solved the problem of becoming a modern Islamic state by choosing democratically to become modern. Turkey has accomplished a breakthrough. Since 1928 Turkey has assimilated the modernity they found useful and kept a free and vital Moslem religion. They have been accepted as a member of NATO. When they are also accepted by the European Community, they will have achieved free and equal understanding between Islam and modernity. This is not about negotiating an agreement, but rather an open understanding between individuals in which every goal may be achieved. Turkey deliberately turned itself into a Western society. The Moslem religion became *a part* of society rather than being *all* of society.

Turkey had for many years been attacked by Kurdish terrorists until the terrorists threatened the ability of the Turkish nation to function. The headquarters of the Kurdish terrorists was in Damascus, Syria, which borders Turkey. Turkey moved its troops to the border with Syria, and told Syria to move the terrorists out. The Taliban refused such a demand in Afghanistan, but Syria hurriedly acquiesced. The Turks captured the terrorist leader when he was ejected, and he is now in jail in Turkey. The rest of the Kurdish terrorists seem to believe that Turkey will do whatever it takes to exterminate them. They are now very quiet. Perhaps they will learn that they have more to gain by cooperating with Turkey than terrorizing it. They have learned something about the terrorist mind that we didn't learn in the United States until September eleventh: A government that gives safe haven to terrorists is responsible for what those terrorists do, or threaten to do, to other nations.

You may remember the attacks on Turkey by the human rights organizations and foreign academics at that time. The government, they said, was the terrorist; the Kurds were freedom fighters.

That brings us to the losers—Iraq and Libya. Only armed force will change the terrorist mind in those countries. They leave me nothing useful to offer.

Chapter 38

Asian Victors

I mentioned in the last chapter that there were huge differences between Arabic Moslem states and non-Arabic Moslem states. Indian and Asian Moslem states have a foundation of modernity to build upon. Also, the Saudi Wahhabi revolution against modernity has had less time to develop there. Indonesia, India, the Philippine Islands, and Malaysia are good examples.

Indonesia

Islam exists all around the world. But the country with the most Moslems in the world is Indonesia. The government is being threatened by the growth of fanatical Moslems obsessed with the need to make everyone follow the rules of the Koran.

In Indonesia, the Saudi Arabians, with unending supplies of money and the prestige of the holy center of Mecca, are trying to indoctrinate the Moslem people with the Saudi Wahhabi brand of terrorist Islam.

Islam originally came to every country it rules through conquest, with one exception. In Indonesia it came through the early trade routes. President Sukarno of Indonesia secularized the government, keeping it from becoming a communist or an Islamic state. However, terrorists are now attacking in Indonesia. In the first truly free election, held in 1999, voters overwhelmingly voted for secular government.

India

India has the second largest number of Moslems. They are feeling the Moslem terror, but fortunately Moslems are a minority of Indian citizens. The Islamic faith and the Hindu faith are polar opposites. While the Koran is the faith of Moslems, Hinduism has no bible, no heresy. Hinduism is tolerant of others. It does not claim to be the only true religion. Hindus claim that all ways of faith are valid and that belief is a personal matter.

I was in India with a partner who has worked on aid projects with me. We were there checking on shipments of rice to India—to see how much good they were doing. The rats were doing very well. In one location we found a mountain of rice dumped on the ground and exposed to the weather. All creatures were eating it, but the humans were losing out.

It's very nice to want to give food to someone poor and hungry and less educated than you are. Often times it works out just as you wish, but you have to be careful. Like a psychologist, you can be helpful, but if you're wrong, it could be more detrimental than any help you might be able to give.

I thought about the rice farmers in Texas who donated the rice, how they thought their hard work was going to help starving people.

I thought about those loading the ship, and the sailors putting a little more effort into moving their precious cargo halfway around the world. I grieved for the Indians and the sailors and the farmers and my partner. He is related to the largest land owner in Kashmir where crops are destroyed by the Moslem terrorists from Pakistan. It is the scene of a fight over land with Pakistan. In Kashmir they really needed food and had the means to successfully distribute it.

Pakistani terrorists have been trying to force India to give up the land through murder attempts on India's parliament. That hardly ever works. They should agree to settle their dispute without the use of terror. And, by God, I think they just might do it. That would be a happy story.

The Philippine Islands

I was introduced to the Philippine Islands by Benjamin Salvosa, a member of the family of General Marcos, the president of the Philippines. General Marcos, although the head of a graft-ridden government, was also dedicated to destroying the Communist terrorists. He sent Benjamin out to scour the world for an honest consultant, and Benjamin picked me.

In the 1970s I was working for a project to build roads in the Philippine Islands. I tried to figure out how the people were thinking. Then I presented my plan to the cabinet. I proposed that the roads be built in short segments by local people. (There were 84 separate native languages along the length of the road.) We used local materials, and the oxen used for farming were prefect soil compactors. If local people controlled the project and the government didn't, my plans usually succeeded. The road was a success.

I brought back a bolo—a short version of the curved Islamic sword. Very sharp, very wicked. It was used by the Moslems of Mindanao, the farthest south of the Philippine Islands. It was the only island conquered by Islam. At that time the Moslems just wanted to be left alone. When the central government tried to enter into their lives, there was trouble—an enduring, dangerous people.

Now, however, things have changed. The Moslems in the Philippines have found it easier to become terrorists. They have become allied with Osama bin Laden. They kidnap moderns and hold them for ransom. It's a sad degradation of a once proud Moslem people. But this is an opportunity for the United States to help the Philippine government. We have done so with special anti-terrorist troops. Now we need to go beyond that to help with education. I once taught economics there at Baguio University. At that time the Filipinos boasted the highest percentage of college graduates in the world. The young people were insatiable for learning and capable of assimilating advanced studies. The Philippines could be the key to modernity facing down the Wahhabi revolution in Asia.

Malaysia

Malaysia's prime minister, Mahather Mohammed, has handled the Saudi Arabian revolution of hatred by building a vibrant modern and prosperous economy and routinely throwing terrorists in jail. Malaysia is the peninsula running down to Singapore. Its largest city, Kuala-Lumpur, has the tallest building in the world. Young women can walk down the streets wearing short shorts. The population is Malay, Hindu, and Chinese. The Moslem Malays make up the majority of the country, which is run by Chinese from Singapore. The Chinese have brought real prosperity to the country and own most of the businesses. By law, to start a company, you have to have a Malay co-owner. It works out in practice. The Chinese are enormously wealthy. Many keep apartments in London for whenever they might visit.

However, walking down the street today, burqas are not uncommon, Prime Minister Mahather needs to see the reality of what is happening on the street. An old Malay Moslem driving down the street with me said, "Piety does not come from burqas, but from individual prayer. Wahhabis take my warning."

Prime Minister Mahather (a Moslem) spent some time with President Bush, in person and on the phone, explaining how he manages to keep terrorists out of Malaysia in spite of the Saudi Arabian pressure for him to embrace the Islamic brand of terrorism. It's simple, he said, "I throw terrorists in jail, one at a time." His government's goal is to show that Islam and modernity are not incompatible. That is my goal in writing this book as well.

Malaysia has thirteen counties. Over the years the government has won the votes in eleven, with only two giving their votes to the Islam of Saudi Arabia. In the last election, however, terrorist Islam controlled votes in three counties—a cause of some concern.

These have been my personal experiences of the rejection of modern thought in Islamic countries in the last twenty-five years. Western thought has been driven out by a terrorist mind-set steeped in the Koran and financed by Saudi Arabia.

This personal journey around the Moslem world shows how recent the rise of fanatical Islam is. Christianity in the United States has its own brand of religious fanatics, but their influence has been waning during the rise of Islam's terror. It is clear that we are at war with Moslem terrorists the world over. However, the majority of Moslems are not terrorists. In each Islamic country, the terrorist mind has been partially created by local environments, but it exists in all Islamic countries. For me it began in 1977 and is still going on. I hope that through my experiences you will get a picture of the everyday practical reality of terrorism.

If we look for causes to explain this massive movement of rage throughout Islam, it is easy to point to the Wahhabi fanatics. But there is never just one cause. There are always many. One might say that each individual person is responsible for our war on terrorism. Each of us should *get real* and feel the psychological reality of the terrorist mind. Each Moslem is different. Each modern individual is different. Individual differences are the answer. You and I are the answer.

Chapter 39

Political Islam

The Prime Minister of Malaysia, Seri Dr. Mahathir bin Mohammed, recently made a speech to the Harvard Club. Following are quotes from the speech which reveal the problems any country with a significant fanatical Islamic population will have.

> The emergence of the Islamic Party has resulted in the struggle to build the resilience of the Malays being deflected by the so-called religious imperatives invented by political Islam.
>
> The Malays are deeply religious, but they are not knowledgeable enough about Islam to distinguish between what is Islamic and what is not. Religious piety is highly valued by the Malays but they equate piety with outward appearance and not the true teachings of the Al-Quran and the true tradition or Hadith of the Prophet. This simple perception of their religion opens opportunities for the unscrupulous to exploit religion for their own purpose.

Religion is not a matter of common sense. It is a matter of belief, of faith. Trying to argue on the basis of common sense or logic is not going to get one anywhere.

But if it is the true teachings of religion it does not matter if it is logical or not. Islam, for example, teaches only good things, good values which can ensure Moslems become good people and their society is stable, well-governed, and prosperous. The fundamentals of Islam can help build a successful and healthy civilization. This was what happened to the ignorant Arabs who embraced Islam 1400 years ago. These wild, unprincipled, feuding Arab tribes united and developed a Moslem civilization which lasted 1300 years. It collapsed only after the Moslems deviated from the true teachings and returned to their pre-Islamic, ignorant Jahilliah ways.

In Malaysia today we are seeing the abuse of the teachings of Islam. Using Islam as its name and shamelessly misinterpreting it, the politicians of the so-called Islamic Party have cashed in on the deep faith of the Malay Moslems to trap them and close their minds to anything else other than what they have been taught by these politicians.

For example, it is normal for people to be grateful for what they get. In Malaysia the development brought about by the Malay-dominated Government must surely earn the thanks and therefore the support of the Malays.

Seeing this, the religiously trained teachers in the Islamic Party actually taught their captive followers, including children in the kindergarten, not to be thankful to the people who gave them anything. They are taught that in Islam there is no need to thank the Government which helps them. They are taught that this is the duty of Government and any Government would do this. They have only to be thankful to Allah and not to the Government for the bounties that they get.

This is totally against the teachings of Islam, but such is the faith in these political Islamic leaders and their interpretations of Islam that the recipients of Government help will actually curse and condemn the very Government which had been generous to them.

On the other hand, any obvious misdeeds by these so-called Moslem politicians is justified or forgiven or overlooked. Thus their leaders can commit khalwat, or surreptitiously marry outside the country, or curse and swear or claim that Allah also curses and swears, even expose themselves to women, or break up the Malay Moslem community by having separate prayers, threatening to divorce their wives should their wives reject their unprincipled behavior, or support other parties, rejecting imams on political grounds through boycotts of any villager who does not support them, but still their leaders will be considered as good Moslems whom they must follow.

Democracy is mainly about the people choosing the Governments to rule the country. It is assumed that the people will choose the good people, the right people who can form a good Government, delivering to the people both their material and spiritual needs, developing the country, and defending the country against foreign hegemony. But sometimes the majority of the people may not be able to choose wisely because they have been completely brainwashed.

In Malaysia many of the Malays have had their minds controlled through the abuse of religious teachings. Today in Malaysia many Malays, not really understanding Islam, have been misled by the seemingly pious turban and Arabic dress of the Islamic Party leaders. They fanatically follow the dictates of this party even when this leads to the country becoming misgoverned, to practices and values against the teachings of Islam. It is not far-fetched to say that for many Malays their Malay and Islamic values have been destroyed. Such is the deviation from Malay and Islamic culture that many Malays are willing to vote and support a Party which advocates and practices violence, which curses and swears, and is led by immoral leaders. The end result of the deviation must be the election of a bad Government and the stoppage of the efforts to ensure that the Malays remain politically empowered and economically as advanced as the other races.

Malaysia is committed to Democracy. We are not liberal democrats but we certainly uphold the most important element of democracy, the right to elect our Governments through voting into power the party we think will best serve us. But because of what I have mentioned regarding the brainwashing of the so-called Islamic Party, there is every danger of the wrong party being elected and forming the Government. We have seen this happening in many countries where populist parties which promise all kinds of impossible things have been elected by a gullible electorate. It is possible for this to happen to Malaysia. It is entirely possible for all the prosperity, the stability, and the racial harmony to be destroyed.

The dilemma that the Malays and the peoples of Malaysia face is whether we should, in the name of democracy, allow the country to be destroyed or we ensure that people are not subjected to manipulations to the point where they will use democracy to destroy democracy.

Chapter 40

The Ways We Think

After talking to people from all over the world and listening to neighborly conversations, I am convinced that most of us have begun to live in a new kind of practical reality. We are not so much afraid that we personally will be killed, rather we have been jolted out of the illusion that everything in our country is as it should be, that we can concentrate on making money while the police protect our safety and dedicated civil rights representatives look after the poor and oppressed. That has never been the practical reality of our lives. It has always been a mirage.

I don't believe that government and human rights activists can protect us. At a gut level, we understand that we live in a world where danger can materialize and kill us at any time, in any number of ways. The practical reality is that we must always fight forces of evil.

For instance, media outlets tell us daily that partisan politics are important in our lives. But we know that partisan politics is one of society's games—it is about someone winning and someone losing rather than about surviving in a dangerous world.

So what is our practical reality? We don't often put it in words: It is the vulnerability of our transportation systems; it is poisoning the local water supply; it is hospitals without enough smallpox vaccine for every person in the community; it is the threat posed by anthrax and other types of biological and chemical weapons; it is the danger of unprotected electricity sources and nuclear power plants.

These, I think, are some of the unspoken and even unconscious feelings that most people have about the practical realities of living with terrorism. Yes, it is a starker world. If our friends want to quibble with us about our policies in this war on terrorism, that's fine, as long as they realize that the whole world is now living with terrorism.

As for what happens around the world, I don't think we pay too much attention to what the media or government says. We are not as interested in abstract theories; we are more focused on the practical reality of what is happening anywhere on our earth.

Palestine is a good example. For some time now, we accepted that the plight of the Palestinians was dire, and that we should be doing something to try to alleviate it. More recently, however, this attitude is changing.

Despite attempts to play down the ecstatic dancing in the streets of Palestine at the news of September eleventh, there are other signs that something is wrong. Seventy thousand people filled a Gaza stadium to cheer a reenactment of that massacre. Americans are waking up to the reality that the Palestinians are not acting this way because they are downtrodden. There is something else at work here.

It reminds me of another time in Europe when the Nazi SS would kill thousands of Jews in a day and then go off for an evening's celebration. We denounced them as evil.

Moslem countries that desire modernity exist. Why does the world ignore them? They hold out an opportunity to bring Moslems and modern people together as partners in defeating terrorism.

Chapter 41

Hatred's Doom

While there were questions about how Pearl Harbor happened, no one pursued them. Our world had been turned upside down. We were at war. Now we are in a new kind of war. Our world has again been turned upside down. We don't even need the government to tell us how to fight this war. We can each choose to become a better person. We don't have to trust the government to tell us how to do that, but the government had better trust us to fight this war one on one.

That is why this book is for individuals. Today modernity rules the world not by armed force but by inclusion. Today the individual residents on our planet can make life as good as possible for each other by implacably destroying the terrorist mind. We may be different as individuals, but we can all get better in our different ways. Our differences open life to all sorts of possibilities—make it richer. They are the answer to a more vibrant future.

Everyone involved in this war is a human being. That doesn't mean we are all alike. It means we are all different. Yet we are still left with the question of why it seems that Moslems produce international terrorists and modern people don't? This is a complex subject with many twists and turns, but it boils down to self-hate expressed by fanatic Moslems that has been taught to them. If we taught our children such enmity, we would have about the same number of terrorists as they do. We know, as a matter of fact, that some moderns do become terrorists even though they may have been taught inclusive diversity and love.

We recognize that Islam has lived through 1400 years without developing the visual arts to explore human feelings. The Wahhabi imams even suppress music. Modern poetry only arose from such bards as Homer, who put their words to music. Islam and modernity must share their art. In a letter to *The New York Times*, Wade Newman had this to say:

> What is the role of the arts in the present crisis? In other words, what kind of art will provide us with solace, memorialize our heroes and translate humanity's hopes and fears into lasting works of beauty?
>
> Not paintings from the private universes of their individual creators that fail to communicate universal meanings. Not scrap-metal sculptures welded into abstract heaps that resemble poor imitations of our recent ruins. Not atonal music compositions, not confessionalist free-verse poetry and not plotless fiction.
>
> We are suddenly faced with life-and-death issues, next to which the personal rantings of so many artists from the last few decades appear self-centered, vapid and inconsequential.

Each of us can create art that overwhelms hatred by living alongside of one another with respect for our differences. We can be angry, but not at anyone or any country or any religion—we can be angry without objects for our anger. We must be inclusive in the way we think and act. That means we love individual people, not ideologies or religions or social systems.

Islam and modernity must be trustworthy and know how to trust individuals. We can be better than we are. If we are to win this war against terrorism together, we must first, demonstrably be the best we can—loving, accepting, inclusive, and compassionate. Second, we must bring out of ourselves the ability to fight in honor and trust. These two realities must exist at the same time or we may fail.

Fanatical Moslems glorify the fierce Islamic warriors who always won battles. But today's fanatics have forgotten how to trust and be trustworthy. They have forgotten that Islamic warriors fought in honor and trust. Today these Moslems dream of victory but hate themselves. They exclude compassion and kindness. Mohammed must be uneasy. His present armies do not know how to fight.

X

LITERARY MIND

Chapter 42

Maimonides's Mind

Maimonides was born in Cordoba, Spain in 1135. He was educated by Arabic masters even though he was a Jew and attended the synagogue. This was not the education found in the Madrassas today. First, he was not taught to be a victim. He was accepted as a Jew. He was part of the greatest culture on earth, Islam. He was thought of as a second Moses by the Jews. He revitalized the Jewish language and at the same time was recognized as the greatest Arabic scholar of his time. I think of him in the gardens in the Alcazar in Seville. He is seated by a fountain (still flowing today) surrounded by Arabic, Jewish, and Christian scholars, leading them into a confluence of three cultures in philosophy and poetry, which seems unimaginable today. The 1100s saw the apex of Islamic literature. At the time it was called The Golden Age.

Maimonides was certainly not a victim. He didn't hate. He lived among beautiful surroundings in a culture of serenity which nurtured a visual art that was expressed abstractly. Christian statues and historical representations were considered too primitive. If you have been to Spain and spent any time at the Alhambra, or Alcazar (the castle) of Seville, or its many cities, you may have felt you had stepped into paradise. There could be no hatred or self-hatred here. There were no feelings of impotence or humiliation. The cultural atmosphere encouraged self-confidence and trust, not the need to defend and betray found in the Islamic world today. What has happened to the Islamic mind since then? It has stagnated in the last 800 years. Western mind has moved on and left it behind.

Maimonides recognized the extreme reliance of the Moslem faith on abstract, logical consistency. It had made possible Islam's success in converting much of the civilized world. But in the end, it would reach its limits. In his most important work, *The Guide for the Perplexed*, he seeks to harmonize philosophy and spirituality in literature. The next two hundred years after his death saw a remarkable confluence of Arab, Jewish, and Christian scholars interacting to create one literature for the world. We have seen nothing like that kind of cultural cooperation since.

It would be another four hundred years before virtual literary reality was discovered in the modern world. And, just think, Maimonides had no understanding of the reality of the novel! If he had, today we might have a new Maimonides writing books for Islamic, Jewish, and modern children alike—perhaps a Robert Louis Stevenson or a Tolkein combined with the world view of Maimonides.

Remember that Islam was the outstanding literary power when Maimonides lived. The Jews and Christians were slaves to a benevolent power in Spain. But by 1492 Islam had completely disappeared from Spain. The Moslems had either left or been slaughtered. They would not stay to become the slaves of Christianity. The Jews did, publicly forsaking their ancient religion, even though it had been the womb out of which the other two religions had sprung. They fled or converted to Christianity or were consumed by the Inquisition.

Chapter 43

Modern Islamic Literature

There are Moslems in twenty-two countries around the world. But 2002 A.D. is not a new Golden Age of Literature. Within the Islamic nations, less than half of the people can read. Arabs, after 1400 years, still communicate mainly by speaking.

A century ago there were few Arabic books besides the Koran. Today, books in Arabic generally offer people abstract information. The preponderance of all books in print are copies of the Koran. Non-Moslem books are routinely banned by the state. The reasons for censorship are indecency, immorality, political theory. More books are banned, burned, or confiscated than are purchased. And the biggest problem for its literature is the assassination of its authors.

Suzanne Mubarak worked diligently for literature in Egypt. The government supported her efforts, but writers were assassinated by Moslem terrorists. Just the threat of assassination is enough to discourage most writers. Nawal al Saadawi, perhaps the most popular

Egyptian writer, fled to the United States after receiving death threats from terrorists. However, she is now back and living in Cairo.

Written Arabic is logical and abstract. It is ancient and intricate, with archaic syntax and vocabulary. Turkey replaced the florid embellishments of Arabian letters with a latin script used in the West, and literature flourished there.

Most Moslems who read at all, read newspapers—short sentences, few and simple words. That is not literature. Despite various dialects, the Moslem religion encourages the acceptance of one language. Translating the Koran is not authorized.

Literature allows the mind to grow. Terrorist minds have been stunted and cannot grow. What is needed is a new Golden Age of Literature that combines Islam and modern thinkers.

In the 1100s, Maimonides was a Jew. In his time in Spain, Jews had more freedom to be the best they could be than under the Christians who followed. In 1492 Queen Isabella of Spain began the Inquisition which sent Spanish Jews fleeing over the world. Where in Islam are Jews tolerated today, much less celebrated, as they were in Islam eight hundred years ago? What happened to the Jews? It is a sad story. At the height of the Jewish death camps under the Nazis, Hitler sent operatives to Islamic countries, and especially to Palestine, to rally them to the German cause. The reaction of many Palestinians to the Jewish death camps was glee. For some time after the war they were still influenced by Nazi philosophy. We need a new Maimonides.

Chapter 44

More than an Army

Women and children are our greatest assets in the war against terrorism. Where women are able to expand their minds, there will always be enough to teach children. If they need books and paper, we can supply books and paper. We can also encourage and support, teaching by example—love, equality, forgiveness, inclusion of diversity, trust. Teach Readin, Ritin, and Rithmetic, but stress inclusion instead of exclusion. The majority of Moslems need to see that the victimhood, hatred, and humiliation that is drummed into boys in the Madrassas, holds no future for the Islamic culture.

That seems a tall order for teachers. We'll need volunteers to help the women and mothers become teachers. Here's a thought. We have many charitable organizations anxious to help, and how about the teachers' unions—instead of giving money to politicians, give some to fight terrorism. I'll bet there would be volunteers for this risky task from all quarters. Volunteers have a lot of freedom to teach in desperate circumstances in Islamic countries.

Of course, we will have to improve our own schools—lead by example again. The occasional teacher will have to give up hatred and victimhood. Don't tell me that there are no American teachers at some time who haven't had a little trouble with self-hatred and self-pity.

In my work in the Islamic nations around the world I have seen many Madrassas. They are usually connected to a mosque and teach that anyone who is not Islamic is the enemy. I remember one young boy saying, "Any country that is not Moslem is our enemy. The United States is our enemy so we must destroy it." Chilling, isn't it?

The Madrassas are our competition in Islam. They feed, clothe, and teach the boys. (Girls are not educated.) The biggest concentration of such schools is in Pakistan. Remember when I escaped from Pakistan in 1977 at the beginning of the book? The Madrassas had already been in Pakistan since the 1950s. Children who had been through those schools made up the army that deposed the elected president, Ali Bhuto. These religious schools exist in almost every country in the world—the United States, Malaysia, Indonesia, India, Bosnia, and all through the Middle East.

Thomas Friedman in *The New York Times* published this quote from a Pakistani writer, Izzat Majeed:

> We Moslems cannot keep blaming the West for all our ills. . . . The embarrassment of wretchedness among us is beyond repair. It is not just the poverty, the illiteracy and the absence of any commonly accepted social contract that define our sense of wretchedness; it is, rather, the increasing awareness among us that we have failed as a civil society by not confronting the historical, social and political demons within us. . . . Without a reformation in the practice of Islam that makes it move forward and not backward, there is no hope for us Moslems anywhere. We have reduced Islam to the organized hypocrisy of state-sponsored mullahism. For more than a thousand years Islam has stood still because the mullahs, who became

de facto clergy instead of genuine scholars, closed the door on "ijtehad" (reinterpreting Islam in light of modernity) and no one came forward with an evolving application of the message of the Holy Koran. All that the mullahs tell you today is how to go back a millennium. We have not been able to evolve a dynamic practice to bring Islam to the people in the language of their own specific era. . . . Oxford and Cambridge were the "madrassas" of Christendom in the 13th century. Look where they are today—among the leading institutions of education in the world. Where are our institutions of learning?

Holy Prophet Muhammad, on returning from a battle, said: "We return from little Jihad to greater Jihad." True Jihad today is not in the hijacking of planes, but in the manufacturing of them.

A few months later, the president of Pakistan, General Musharraf, was caught between the American threat to withhold aid and the Indian threat of a war. He decided to accept reality rather than keep trying to uphold Islamic terrorism.

He said, "Do we want Pakistan to become a theocratic state? Do we believe that religious education alone is enough for governance, or do we want Pakistan to emerge as a dynamic Islamic state? The verdict of the masses is in favor of a progressive Islamic state."

We don't want to cheer what is only speech, but who knows? Government-backed schools in Pakistan, teaching literature and science without hatred, is a bigger victory in the war on terrorism than is the defeat of the Taliban. It has happened without violence, just the courage of General Musharraf. He has also pledged to abolish the terrorist training camps in the Pakistan-controlled regions of Kashmir. Hopefully the Madrassas, teaching the Koran and hate, will be on the way out. You and I can help President Musharraf with his educational problems. Volunteers in education might be mightier than any army.

Chapter 45

Islam Together with Modernity

Islamic terrorism has taken twenty-five years to develop, and it will take many more years for modern people and Moslems to join together to fight a terrorism that is our common enemy.

Literature can be our ally in this war because literature is inclusive. It is also individual. An individual writes about a reality. Another individual reads it and creates a reality of her own in her own mind. If the writing describes a desert she will create her mental reality of a desert in which she lives and breathes. No reader's reality of the desert is like another's. If a person reads many books they will each become a multiple reality.

A Moslem reader can share words of multiple reality with a modern reader so the distinctions between the two cultures shrink. Terrorist qualities such as self-hatred, self-delusion, and humiliation are perceived in terms of psychological reality. They can thus be shared between Moslems and the modern world. Many Moslems think terrorism is a mistake and want to learn from modernity. Even in Iran, there were as many meetings by moderate Moslems expressing sorrow and support for the United States on September 11, 2001, as there were celebrating it. How do we reach these potential allies against terrorism? Good literature is one way. I have mentioned one of my books, *Beyond Literacy*, which is being translated into Iranian. May I tell you one of the dark secrets of the publishing industry? Advertising does little to sell books. A book sells because one person tells another about it. Moderns and Moslems must buy each other's books. Tell a friend!

Publishing in the Islamic world is difficult. We need more modern books translated into Arabic. Presently Harry Potter books by J. K. Rowling are being translated into Arabic, plus a few other titles. Most of the others are information books. But this is only true in the Arab Moslem countries. India and Asian Moslem countries do not have the same censorship and anti-modern problems. This is where a new modern literary revolution can take on the Wahhabi revolution.

Every country that is not a Moslem country, but has Moslem immigrants, should be sure that Moslems get more books in Arabic to read. There is a movement to get charitable giving of books under way. We could all buy a few modern books in Arabic for local Moslem schools.

Moslem books translated into modern languages are plentiful. Nawal El Saadawi books are available, plus Raja Shehadeh, and hundreds of other writers. Look in the appendix for a list of books. This is our opportunity to buy Moslem books to support the literary revolution against Wahhabi fanaticism.

Chapter 46

Pay Attention to the Children

I started this book on September 11, 2001, when my wife Joan and I were in London talking with Jane Spender of London PEN (Poetry, Essays, Novels) International about international literary awards for young people. That day it seemed to me that literary awards could be a powerful weapon in the war on terrorism. I'm putting the finished book down a year later. Hopefully it will be published in 2003. I believe even more strongly now that international literary awards will be useful in bringing Islam and modernity together.

PEN, the international society of writers, was established by George Bernard Shaw and some friends in 1921. One of PEN's functions has been to defend writers all over the world imprisoned by the state for what they write. The United States, as well as other countries, have imprisoned writers for just those reasons.

The Mid-Eastern Islamic states have fewer PEN chapters than other parts of the world. This is too bad, because it is the one place in the world where literature would do the most good. The problem for PEN is finding a group of writers to open a PEN center which could remain independent and not be brought under the control of fanatical Wahhabi-like states.

PEN centers give national literary prizes each year for excellent writing. There is a move to give young beginning writers literary prizes on an international scale. It would be a grand move if PEN International took it on. Getting young people to communicate about literature, could be one of the most important efforts to curb terrorism. Each of us can contribute to such a program.

One of the foundations of any community is how young people organize and express language. PEN Texas has been involved since 1995 in the development of an approach to effective writing which could be called "the sport of writing." This sport recognizes winners. In Texas it holds a writing competition in high schools, choosing winners in poetry, the essay, and the novel. The Language Art teachers of the winning students receive an award for coaching writing.

School systems should recognize that involving students in the sport of writing can reap benefits for the community. Treating effective writing as a sport improves all kinds of school work and community participation. As an environment for teaching, it affects the way young brains develop. It is hard to hate in such an environment. As other sports do, it improves self-confidence. Even though there is only one winner, all who participate become part of the team.

The sport of writing casts the teacher as a coach. The goal is to win. Grammar, like the basic moves in a sport, is fundamental and absolutely necessary, but it doesn't win the award. The ability to bring the reader's sight, smell, and hearing into the writer's world wins the award. The writer must create a partnership with the reader. And that means the writer's language must evoke concrete feelings of reality.

The final PEN Texas competition is statewide and brings the attention of the entire state to the value of writing. We see whole families from all over the state accompanying their competitors. No football team has as loyal a following as these young writers.

PEN Texas does not offer children monetary awards for poetry, essays, and novels, but rather a private mentoring relationship with a successful writer. One might think that recognizing children's writing was a pointless activity with the people of our country threatened daily and hourly by death from unseen terrorists. But I am arguing that paying attention to the children of the world is the way to defeat the terrorists.

One of my arguments was presented in a new book by Margaret Meek, *Children's Literature and National Identity*. It asks how a baby knows that he is English, German, or some other nationality. Margaret is one of the leaders of a movement in the European Community to create more flexible national identities—where the child can be English and also include German influences, or others. This is how children can become a part of Europe through literature. You have to start with young people, and Margaret and her group of diverse professors have made measurable progress. I felt that our Texas method of awarding prizes to children for their writing would add extra energy to the endeavor.

So, as I mentioned earlier, I'm trying to sell Jane Spender on the idea of international awards for children's writing. Jane is the director of the international office of PEN in London, but there are chapters in most countries.

Immediately, however, an issue arose: In one generation, childhood literature in Palestine had produced a national identity of children who (1) know they are victims, (2) hate Jews, and (3) will commit suicide in order to kill as many Jewish men, women, and children as possible. Some of these warriors of hate are as young as seven years old. Palestinians are just an example. The percentage of the population under seventeen years may be as high as 80 percent in the Islamic world. If you catch them at the right age, it takes only about four years to fill an innocent child with hatred. There are countries all over the world where children's literature, both printed and oral, is creating people who hate and wish to kill. You have to be carefully taught to accomplish that.

Yet the PEN award had to be international. This was the stalemate on September 11, 2001, when the World Trade Center was attacked. It delayed the possibility of an international award for children. How could we include countries training their children to hate? There is only one answer. Islamic women must heal their children's hatred. They don't have to change their culture. They have a great cultural heritage. And it can prosper where openness and diversity are allowed in. Children cannot go to the Madrassas. Their mothers can learn to teach them and become proud of them—their gift to a future where Islam and modernity can learn from each other.

After September eleventh, I felt other things were more important, like orienting myself to live in a new world. But perhaps nothing is more important than healing children's hatred. I know from experience the healing energy that can be generated in children by the opportunity to win an award. "Win" is the significant word here. It can be like an opportunity to become a movie star or a hero. It can even compete with—and beat—becoming a suicide bomber. This is not a fantasy. It can be presented to children as an opportunity to give their talents to the world instead of their hatred. Now that my book on the terrorist mind is complete, I hope, at last, to begin working on this project. You are invited to join in. Help save the world! While this is not an official PEN program, members of PEN know more about literature than most people. Some PEN chapters from around the world are listed in the appendix.

XI

TRUSTING MIND

Chapter 47

The World Has Changed

There is a stone house isolated on the African shore of the Mediterranean: two stories high and rambling over the side of the mountain. Imagine Osama bin Laden in a large room of the house. He is nursing a new scraggly beard.

To escape from Afghanistan, he had to shave his beard and hair and don blue jeans and a short leather coat. At the moment, however, he wears a long white robe and a turban. He is surrounded by twenty-six similarly garbed men—one from each of the twenty-two Moslem states and one each from Bosnia, Germany, Spain, and the United States. They are sitting on cushions that rest on a floor three layers deep with costly Persian rugs.

Osama bin Laden has always been a man of power, but now he is the mystical Robin Hood of Islamic terror. His eyes gleam as he speaks.

"You see how easy it was—two office buildings down, three thousand people killed at the cost of a handful of suicide martyrs now enjoying the delights of heaven. That single operation has brought the United States to its knees. Look at them, quaking in their boots, their economy in disarray. No one trusts the business leaders. No one trusts the government. No one trusts their health care system. And most pitiful of all, no one trusts the religious leaders. In fact, no one trusts anyone else."

The other members of the meeting are moved and stand on their feet to show their support. Osama bin Laden stands also and strides among them.

"They are toppling. I tell you now is the time to plan a more devastating attack, and another, and another. They will crumble. We have the weapons of mass destruction and we can breed all the martyrs we need to deliver them. Who can stop us? Our friends in Europe feel the same way."

Hold it! You and I know this is all nonsense. This scene is imaginary.

It may have seemed that we lacked trust in ourselves *before* September eleventh, but since that pointless terrorist atrocity, Americans have become galvanized. The United States may have suffered the loss of citizens, but the country became stronger, not weaker. Among the discordance of different races, the rich and the poor, and divided partisan politics, our country has emerged with awesome potential.

We know now that we face an enemy with the means and the will to destroy our country. But the terrorists are also on notice: We see you, we know who you are. As Lincoln said, we are a country of the people, by the people and for the people, and we will not perish from this earth.

I have talked to many people across the country since the attack. Striking to me are the many African Americans, often raised to think of themselves as alienated, who say, "They have attacked *us*, all of us Americans. They have made a big mistake." It may not be obvious, but we are becoming a united country of Rosie the Riveters, last seen in World War II. Our government has acted. We have as a nation declared war on terrorism.

We all know that our world has changed. Now, each and every one of us must change as well. We must trust one another to do the right thing, the honest and honorable thing. As a body, we will fix what we haven't trusted. Look at the stock market and see what we Americans think. We're not kidding. Business had better be trustworthy very quickly. And we will judge business in the stock market. What the government does is not overwhelmingly important. But the government better clean up its act as well. We're at war and we don't have time for petty politics.

In this new world every one of us is important and needed. Remember, all Jesus needed was twelve disciples. In our everyday living and working, we each touch at least twelve others in meaningful ways. This new world where we live—warriors in the war against terror—demands that we trust each other.

Chapter 48

Warriors

Don McComber comes out of the generation of national business leaders that led the United States before the modern period. His experience goes back to World War II. Today, he is helping me focus on the quality of trust in our country.

"Look, Don, think about how similar the attacks on Pearl Harbor on December 7, 1941, and on the World Trade Center in 2001 are! Both attacks involved the deaths of a small number of the enemy (100 Japanese in 1941 and 19 terrorists in 2001) and resulted in the deaths of thousands of U.S. citizens (2200 at Pearl Harbor and 2800 in New York). In both cases, everyone in the country felt the horror and suffering of the families of the victims. In World War II, we rose together in trust and became a unified nation. I believe that is happening to us today."

Don says, "That trust made it possible for the United States to dominate business throughout the whole world after the war. I was there. I know that it was hard-won trust in one another that created that success. Also, I know that we have been losing that trust. Trust isn't a gift. People say nowadays, 'Oh, I trust my family, my friends.' But families are betrayed, friends betray. Young people don't even know what the word means."

Don is getting excited. "At the time of World War II, a man who went bankrupt was not only temporarily ruined, he was apt to be ruined for life. He couldn't be trusted! Nowadays there are more than a million bankruptcies each year. People run up credit-card debt and then go bankrupt. They think that's smart. They have no concept of trust. For them, there is nothing to trust.

"And this is something Congress can't fix. We must individually find a trust that will save us—one person at a time. You think we're doing so well now, fixing all the things wrong with us? Well, it's a good beginning. Will we have the stamina to see it through? I'm not as sure as you seem to be. Let me put this in the simplest terms: Can we do what we say we will do? Just start with that. The Afghan foreign minister says the United States is the only country that has done what it says it will do. That's fine, but things are going to get much harder.

"I understand how this ties into the war on terrorism. Trust is absolutely necessary. But I don't think you have considered the terrorist mind sufficiently. That's what your book is about.

"It could go either way. Do you realize that? Let's hope there are enough good people in the United States and in Islam who can trust each other. If there are not, this may be another war we lose."

Don puts his hand on my shoulder as I get up to leave, "You're headed in the right direction, Pat. Even though I'm long retired, I'm going to be working to bring mutual trust back to the hospital system. We're going to be needing that in this new world."

Don McComber is a warrior. And this new world will need lots of warriors.

Each one of us can find different ways to forge mutual trust between Islam and modernity. In the next chapters you will find aspects of trust that we can all use. They are ways that we can live in trust, but they are not easy.

Chapter 49

Trust

Consider this terrorist. He is unable to trust anyone. He hauls his luggage onto the plane himself, not trusting the baggage system. He wants receipts for every purchase. He won't trust his coat to a coat rack in a restaurant. When he orders food, he wants a detailed guarantee of how a dish will be prepared. In the Islamic world, it seems no one is trustworthy. A foe today may be a friend tomorrow, and then a foe again on another day. My terrorist finds that so ordinary that he doesn't comment on it. It's what he expects.

One of the best indicators of a terrorist mind is this lack of ability to trust. The best defense against terrorists is to live in a society that can trust. There the terrorist is highlighted.

Get together in communities to fight the war on terrorism. Cities can divide into diverse communities. A community can exist anywhere as long as people know and trust each other. In such a community they will be able to identify possible terrorists in their midst. Terrorists function most effectively only where there is no community.

But are we capable of building these trusting relationships? We'd better learn how to build them if we want to recognize the terrorist mind. We should heed the words of St. Paul:

> *For we struggle not against flesh and blood,*
> *but against principalities, against powers,*
> *against the rulers of the darkness of this world,*
> *against spiritual wickedness in high places.*

Recent polls indicate that people feel overwhelmingly concerned about society's ability to be true. Our dilemma today is that we know that moral rules haven't resulted in trust, and neither have ethical structures nor more constricting laws. My approach to trust makes a critical distinction between what people do and what they think. What a terrorist thinks is even more important than what he does. If we know his mind, we may be able to deter his actions.

We often repress the inclusive reality of right and wrong and blame people for what they do, just as the terrorist does. If we hold terrorists to the standard of being responsible for who they are, we have to hold ourselves responsible for who we are as well. We are afraid to know too much about ourselves. For example, most of us know in our hearts that our religious and political leaders are often not trustworthy in their personal selves. But we, just like the terrorists, find it easier to blame others than to pay attention to reality.

Realistic knowing is a terrible responsibility. Terrorists do not want to know who they are, fearing that underneath their self-hatred there may be nothing. This is a deep fear. It destroys self-confidence. To know might be too much to bear.

People rush to blame the terrorist's actions. But they are afraid to judge the terrorist mind. Why is that? Because it's a whole lot easier to judge an action than it is to judge thinking. But if we don't attempt to judge thinking, we may be killed by the action. Perhaps the hate-crime approach might be more useful: We judge the action in light of the hate. After all, how you think *is* who you are.

Chapter 50

Be Right!

Dogs and children know whom to trust. It seems that only in the childlike reality of being true to yourself can you know whom to trust. Rational thinking is not available to very young children. They think in simple realities. We perceive them as true and innocent. We have had experiences with children when they have *irrationally* disliked someone. We ask, "How could you dislike him? What has he done?" The child has no words to express an ambiguous lack of trust. She *just knows* how she feels. If you can think in simple realities as a child does, perhaps you can find within yourself feelings of right and wrong. You can be true in yourself.

Before a toddler can speak, she knows whom to trust. If she cannot trust a person, she makes it perfectly clear by hiding behind her mother's legs.

As an adult, I attempted to make judgments by applying rules of social behavior. Did this person I was judging have a history of trustworthy behavior? How did I weigh one set of behaviors against another? What were the rules I used for judging these behaviors? This is the reality of discrimination and relevance in highly complex social situations. It was hopeless, I was so often wrong about whom to trust. I finally decided I had no rules to apply to the average person I met.

Now, I know how children do it. Realistic thinking is holistic. It is a compass that points me to specific realities, not to general rules. As I live, true to my own reality, I know holistically who is true to their reality and, therefore, whom to trust. Moreover, this is accomplished in microseconds, leaving me comfortable in social situations. That childhood ability to trust is still felt within me after all the years of repression by abstract thinking.

You *just know* what is right. Knowing right from wrong has been a favorite topic in the literature of the last six hundred years. David Copperfield *just knew* that his mother was about to marry a bad man. He also *just knew* that his aunt was good and to be trusted. He ran away to be with her. Tom Sawyer and his young friends knew who was to be trusted and who wasn't. Yet what they *just knew* was clearly at odds with the rationalizations of their society.

Rules can always be rationalized to hypocritical falsehoods. Be aware that what started out as a realistic thought can be rationalized, but you may still think it is reality.

Life is simply heading in its own direction. It cannot be analyzed or rationalized. We see each individual act in rapidly changing conditions. And it is up to us to discover what is right in each specific circumstance.

Life is a rhythm stirring within you, like deep and easy breathing, that tunes your thoughts to the full continuity of human existence. A recollection surfaces from far within you. You may feel the long ages of human habitation drawing you in, absorbing you, making you part of the same continuity, or you may feel awe in the presence of absolutely knowing what is right in a particular circumstance. Belonging to the continuity of culture is fulfilling. It can happen without any effort on your part. Suddenly you are a part of it. You belong, you respect, you partake, you contribute to all you are. Humanity accepts you; it is a better and safer, an impregnable, security.

People speak different languages and have different kinds of rational thoughts and ideologies. But we all have the same feelings for what is right—even among different religions. Moslems and Christians and Jews feel that there is only one god who wants people to be good. Native Americans, isolated across vast oceans, felt there was a great spirit in the sky.

If you work at something you think is important in reality, you can polish your ability to know what is right. At work, don't give your word or guarantee if you might break it. In your own real world, you can know what is right and what is wrong. Knowing what is right in your own self is the true way of living.

Chapter 51

Trust Yourself

One of the simplest experiences of trust is when you do what you say you will do. This means that in your mind you pledge yourself to do what you say. If you know that you may not be able to do it, you don't say you will. That is the secret of modernity. Islam can understand the words, but not the thinking. Terrorists, full of self-pity and self-hatred, become self-delusional through self-deception. They deceive themselves about the reality of the world, and then the world they inhabit becomes a delusion.

Both Islamic and modern people must begin to depend on self-acceptance, on self-respect, on knowing realistically what is right and what is wrong, on authenticity, on being trusted, on being able to trust.

You know how to think realistically. With that as your guide, you can give up vanity and all the rational illusions of who you are. This time, you're going to get things right.

Being true is personally real; it is absolute. Acting *as though* you are true is relative—with nothing there to trust. We try to use our rational thinking to save ourselves. But rational thought doesn't save us. When reality is repressed, we do things that destroy confidence and self-respect. When we are living at our full potential, reality comes before abstraction.

If you have ever shopped in Moslem countries, you've noticed that a seller of an ancient statue is not concerned with the reality of the statue, only with how much he can get you to pay for it. He sees the *transaction* as reality, not the statue. And his reality of the transaction is a deception. We may think excessive bargaining is cute. But it represents a culture in which lying has become the reality. Whatever one *says* is taken to be reality. Lies become reality. The statue is not the reality. Arafat says he knew nothing about a shipload of arms. If he says it, it is true to him. Do you think you can trust him?

Although we are faced with the dissonance of conflicting cultures, there is a way to be comfortable and serene in the midst of this chaotic state in which we live. We can find a true feeling lodestone, a compass that will always point in a true direction for us personally, no matter how violent the storm. Falseness is what our inner compass points away from.

We are sisters and brothers in the human continuum. The compass can always show us its immutable direction. No matter how things or values change, it will always point to what is true. It can always illuminate the uniquely right thing for you, personally, to do. It transcends all moral rules. You can find confidence and a stable self-respect with this compass.

How can you remain simple and real?

There are basic guides to the problems of a real world. Go back! Trace the continuity of humanity and bring its guides into this complex world of tricks and mirrors, without rationalizing them. You can keep them real just as you have kept your own self real. In your own heart are the simple realities of what is right.

Welcome to a better world! Your modern thinking has allowed you to step through the abstract mirror into a looking-glass world in which dreams, aspirations, hope, the right way, are found—where your life becomes a compass always pointing to what is true! You are now ready to make your own self realistic. That means going beyond abstract rules such as Islam lives by. And this is the best way to help Islam fight its own terrorists, by living in trust yourself.

XII

HOPE'S MIND

Chapter 52

One Person at a Time

President Bush has set up a new approach to communicating with the world, the Office of Global Communications. At first glance, this appears to be moving in the direction of a new public diplomacy for a changed world. Unfortunately, this new public diplomacy is being run by the same people in the State Department and the White House who are running the government's traditional diplomacy. Traditional diplomacy is formulated and organized to be a consistent government policy. This will never work today. Public diplomacy must come from the public, in all its diversity. In this war on terrorism, abstract, rationally consistent policy can only influence governments. The practical reality of life lived on the ground, moment by moment and person by person, can only be transmitted by the public. This book has been written for them.

It was government diplomacy that influenced the fall of the modern Shah of Iran and the beginning of the twenty-year terrorist tyranny of the Islamic revolution there.

It was the United States human rights groups that supported the terrorist groups in Algeria and Tunisia as freedom fighters, even though a hundred thousand people were killed in their rebellions. If they had won, they would have installed nondemocratic governments of repression without freedom for women. But those rebellions failed, and both Tunisia and Algeria are providing modern freedoms.

Recall how the Saudis used our U.S. oil money to help pay for their fanatical Wahabbi revolution through all of Islam. The Saudis encourage suicide bombers in Israel. So our State Department is really saying, "Come on, kick us again. We like it."

Those are just a few examples of our official Mideast government diplomacy. There may be many strategic reasons for a government policy which the public may not dictate, but for God's sake, let's use the Office of Global Communications to encourage public communication that only our diverse public can provide—one person at a time. Ordinary American and Islamic citizens carry our message best.

My 1989 book, *War's End*, was about how individual people had changed the world. That book pointed out a psychological change in the European and Russian public that would lead to the fall of the Berlin Wall and create peace between the warring nations of Europe. A month after the book was published, the Berlin Wall did fall. Individual people had changed, and so the world had changed. There was no more cold war. There was no governmental diplomacy anywhere in the world that could say, "Our policy changed the world." It was the public—the people of Europe and Russia—who changed the world.

The closest explanation (not cause) for this appears in *War's End*. The people of Russia and Europe had changed because reading for pleasure had become a common practice there—the State Department hadn't noticed that. For instance, Russia had tight censorship on reading, but it had good communist schooling that taught everyone to read. What they were reading was not important. What mattered was that *they were reading*. Books, like novels, that reveal a common humanity in all people, make it hard for one country to hate another and go to war with it.

Today the world is very different from the end of the cold war, but still we need a psychological change in people. We don't need ideological squabbles now, we need healing of the good people of Islam and the modern world.

I am indebted to a Malaysian friend for this comment about Moslem moderates as opposed to extremists. "My respect goes unreservedly to these decent men and women, for whom generalization has evidently been a bane. Especially in predominantly non-Muslim jurisdictions, they bear the brunt of their extremist brethren's heinous work. The second group is not quite as benign. If it takes intent coupled with action to make a terrorist, members of this group are halfway there. They are not terrorists per se, but qualify as terrorist apologists. Often educated, affluent, and articulate, these terrorist sympathizers do not have the stomach to perpetrate the offensive act." This comparison applies to human rights activists in the modern West as well as it does to Islamics.

Our allies in Europe may not follow us into necessary fighting in this war on terror, but they will follow us into individual pursuits of everyday life such as sports, literature, music, art, movies—healing hatred through education, health care, and business ventures. We need these kinds of opportunities to establish two-way interactions between diverse individuals. More prizes for excellence in these kinds of activities is what we need in public diplomacy.

Most American cities have organizations that encourage local volunteers to greet and look after foreign visitors. Volunteers take them around the city, often take them into their homes for food and lodging. Friendships can develop. The Houston International Protocol Alliance and the Philadelphia International Visitors Council are two such organizations. Check your city or university, I'll bet you can find a way to participate.

Through my long experience, I must affirm that some countries of the world are anti-American, but the people of anti-American countries can individually have a lot of affection for us personally.

Wouldn't you rather be an individual American rather than an abstract hated-American?

Chapter 53

The War on the War on Terrorism

Anti-Americanism is no longer a mild, general tendency in Europe; it has become, in the war on terrorism, an intellectual principle: United States' power is wrong—our superior wealth, our superior military, our superior education. This kind of thinking also exists in the United States; some people can't see us as being attacked in a war on terrorism, but rather as being responsible for the war. The mere fact of our power makes us the enemy.

Let us be clear, some intellectuals are complicit with the terrorists who threaten you and me. They are at war with our war on terrorism.

Our war on terror is portrayed as a lack of concern for the rights of people in less-advantaged countries. These rights become more important than our war on terrorism. Where we see the liberation of Afghanistan, others see the killing of innocent civilians.

For example, Malaysia is a democracy, but for intellectual activists it is an authoritarian "Asian way" democracy. Wahabbi Moslems are encouraging more burqa-clad women on Malaysian streets, more repression, less freedom. This is perceived by some human rights activists as a victory for democracy rather than a step in the conquest of Malaysia by Wahabbi-inspired terrorists who would destroy freedom in the present modern-oriented Malaysian society.

I've mentioned that my professional background has been in post-modern thinking. Back in the 1990s, Robert Reich as Treasury Secretary was writing, "racial, sexual and age difference will become less important as differences in ability continue to grow." And Alvin Toffler wrote, "The hyper-speed of change today means that given facts become obsolete. Knowledge built on them becomes less desirable." What this means is that new kinds of people were able to live with ambiguity and without such absolutes as an unchanging universal truth. They got real. They could handle ambiguity without resorting to abstract ideology.

This implies an inclusion of diverse people's thinking as conversations among equals. The danger for a nation at war is that inclusion becomes toleration. Thus we might tolerate the terrorist's desire to kill us. Then we would be dead. Or we and our loved ones would live only because we would have included the danger. An aspect of post-modern thinking—that everyone was equal—has led human rights groups to *tolerate* differences in others rather than *including* them in their thinking.

I still think in the post-modern ways of Reich and Toffler, but I choose to accept the responsibility for myself, and others, of staying alive. September eleventh tended to unite the country behind the reality of a new kind of war. It found some post-modern thinkers unable to include a change in the reality of our country and of the world. These are good-hearted, progressive thinkers on the whole. We need them. But the reality is that small hate groups now have the means of mass destruction and the suicidal will to use them against our country.

There may be an unbridgeable chasm between the abstractions of intellectual activists and our simple, realistic war on terrorism. Abstract views have to get real. Some object to our power—not the way we use power, but just the fact that we have power. Our war on terrorism is not as important as our power. What should we do? Commit suicide?

Will this be another war we lose, like Vietnam? There is one big difference: The Vietnamese were not threatening our country. Terrorists are threatening you and me. Will our present war on terror be more like World War II or like Vietnam?

Well, it seems to me that the United States must treat the post-modern, human rights-oriented, democratic, intellectual culture of Europe as I have suggested that it treat Islamic culture—get together with it and find some common ground to pursue our war on terrorism.

We must realize that we are closer to Islam than we are to our post-modern culture's way of thinking. First, Islam is just as threatened by terrorism as we are. Second, post-modern culture feeds on the "power is evil, downtrodden is good" culture of terrorism. It is as mother's milk to them.

Unfortunately, again it seems that reality is not being addressed. Terrorists are not necessarily poor or desperate or downtrodden. The National Bureau of Economic Research has discovered that terrorists tend to be wealthier and better educated than Islamic people in general. And the post-modern human rights culture has little reason to believe that their way of thinking reduces the reality of terrorism.

One solution is to shift away from seeing the world in abstractions and toward feeling the world in reality. If it is pointless to argue about universal abstractions, perhaps we can communicate as one diverse person to another in terms of practical, concrete reality. Is it better to show someone how to fish, or to give them a fish, or to do both? If you show someone how to fish in reality, then he will know how to fish and he will also have a fish. Is it better to be seen as helping people or to know the reality of that help on the ground, in person, one person at a time?

You can show people that you have no power over them because they can always choose to be responsible for themselves. Convince them that it is only in the abstract that you are more powerful than they are. And because they believe you are more powerful, they become victims and utterly dependent on you.

There are no abstract answers to this dilemma; it depends on individual reality. But, at least, here is an area where we my be able to open up the door to individual communication and, eventually, to inclusive thinking.

Chapter 54

Thoughts We Can't Think

There are some thoughts that you can listen to in the abstract, but can't accept as applying to yourself. Although the cause may be *implied*, it can be *logically proven* to you that the effect exists. Nevertheless, in personal reality, you don't think of the abstraction until after experiencing the reality. If you can't feel the reality first, you can only think of it as an abstract thought.

I think you will see what I mean if I tell you about Sherif. I am in a restaurant. My waiter is a bulky Moslem with an air of restrained force. This is Sherif. He has lived in the United States for fifteen years, has a wife and two children. His English is good, almost colloquial. He works two jobs a day and sends most of the money back to his family in Iraq. He says, "Once we were middle class. Now, in Iraq, my family is rich with the money I send. There is just my mother and two sisters. I say to them, 'Here is money. Stay in the house, watch television until I am there personally to tell you what to do.'"

I am amazed. "But Sherif, you have lived here fifteen years. How can you believe that you can tell people thousands of miles away how to behave in the smallest details of their lives? What if they feel an obligation to actively participate in their culture? You can't imprison them with your own will."

Sherif could not hear me. To him it is a given that his women are imprisoned by his will. That is the way it is. His eyes slide over any other way of thinking about it. The Koran says the purity of women is absolute. It is unthinkable that a wife or woman family member could have an affair. She would be stoned to death and forgotten—wiped out of reality.

It seems to me that American Moslems I talk to find the reality of modern sex something they can't think about. They can only think of it in absolutes. The Koran says, as an absolute, unchanging truth, that the female is subject to the man's will.

But Sherif has become aware that there is something here he cannot think about. "Tell me about American women," he says.

"You see, Americans assume that each woman is free to do what she wants. Only she is responsible for her soul," I tell him.

To this, Sherif would answer, "But what she wants is some man to tell her what to do." He cannot even think about what I have said. It has no abstract, unchanging, cause-and-effect meaning.

Moslems believe that we are breeding a wild licentiousness in the modern younger generation—perhaps so, but perhaps not. I look back at the time before World War II when I was a child. I didn't hear about sex as a recreational activity then. Women could vote and could make their own choices about what kind of life they wished to live. Trust was very important then.

Today I ask young people about trust, and they say, "Sure, I trust people."

"But which people?"

"Well, you know, people in general—its the system, you know.

The government takes care of things, so we don't have to worry. We just trust most people."

In my childhood, trust had to be painfully earned. The government didn't guarantee trust in banks, in home loans, or in food for our tables. The heads of most companies began in the lowest jobs and rose in the company because they *could be trusted*. They averaged a C in high school and didn't go to college. What companies were looking for was trust, not IQ. A test for employment could not tell you about trust, so tests were not used. A company's executives were valued because they could sense if a person was trustworthy.

The world did an about-face after World War II. I saw it. Innocence was gone. We gave up trust for progress—the modern world was born, but trust between individuals was lost. After September 11, 2001, the world turned over. Individual trust has suddenly become important again.

I have known Sherif for some time now. This is a restaurant where we often eat. He obviously cannot think in my terms nor I in his. There is no meaningful conversation between us. So I decided to try another avenue. Even though we can't think the same way, maybe we can trust each other.

"Sherif, do you trust me to do what I tell you I will do?"

Still no connection. Sherif struggles with it, "Inshalla."

"Inshalla—if Allah wills it? You mean that I will do what I say if Allah wills it?"

"Yes."

"You mean you can't trust me because it doesn't depend on what I will, but on what God wills? Well, God can't will everything. I think that maybe we can trust each other to do what we individually say we will do. We both know that 99 percent of the time God will not step in at a tornado or a car wreck to keep me from fulfilling what I say I will do. In the practical reality of our lives, we can trust each other *if we choose to*."

After many months of being suspicious, Sherif and I are beginning to routinely trust each other. I've done silly things like surreptitiously adding more coins to his change on a luncheon bill to see if he will give the excess change back to the cashier. He has. Does that mean he is trustworthy? No, but it all adds up. But I still think, even after checking out his trustworthiness, that Sherif is still told by his Koran to conquer me, the infidel.

Sherif has tested my trustworthiness too, but he knows that Americans have been trusting their government instead of each other, and knows that their government cannot protect them as individuals in a terrorist-dominated world. One day he bursts out, "Patton, we have to do something." Then Sherif tells me that he has to be out of town, leaving his family here. He is not living in a Moslem enclave, but in a well-kept, inclusive American neighborhood. He is a little worried. I say that I will be glad to check on them for him while he is gone.

Sherif's skin pales. His eyes jump all over the room. I know what he is thinking, "How can this man who gives his wife the choice of what she will do, look after my wife and children? I can't trust him." Sherif makes an excuse and leaves hurriedly.

However, just before his trip, he comes back hesitantly, "Patton, I wish you would check on my wife. I do trust you. It's a strange feeling, but I do. I feel we must do this thing."

We? I hadn't thought of leaving my wife in the hands of a man who treated women like animals. In similar circumstances, could I ask Sherif to look after my wife? Moslems have contempt for their wives don't they? They are always bossing them around and even beating them. They are also attracted by thoughts of forbidden, wild sex with shameful, unfaithful modern women who can choose for themselves what they will do.

Well . . . it was easy to check on the needs of Sherif's wife and children, who are delightful and showing no signs of being beaten or abused . . . and I guess I might ask him to do the same for me some day. But I will continue checking his trustworthiness, as he will mine. There is no one in the world to guarantee our trust except him and me.

One day recently I happened upon Sherif on the street, and he said, "I've been thinking. Even though we don't think the same way, somehow we do trust one another. That may be the most important thing in the world. You know, this terrorist plague is really just a matter of trust. You and I can start to do something about it. Let's try."

I don't know *if* enough people will come to trust one another, but I know now that enough people *can* trust one another, to make the difference. That's the only way we will win the war on terrorism. We can all live in greatness, trusting reality, teaching children not to hate, learning about each other through literature. I've seen it happen in Turkey and the Philippine Islands. Troops cannot win the war. Only individual Moslems and moderns can do that.

Chapter 55

Extinguishing Terrorism

Let me tell you a story about a woman Moslem writer I have mentioned before. In polite Islamic society, she's called "That Whore"; in impolite society, something much worse.

The writer, Nawal El Saadawi, was born in 1931 in a small town in Egypt and attended local Arab schools. She writes in Arabic for Moslem audiences, yet most of her novels have been translated into other languages. Foreign sales of her books exceed Islamic sales. In the United States, Amazon Books has twenty of her books for sale in English translations. Customer reviews range from 4 to 5 stars (5 being the maximum).

More than any other living Arab writer, she is able to express simply the mysticism of the Arab culture. Both dialect and formal Arabic mingle in her stories so that Arabian readers who do not grasp the difficult grammar of formal Arabic are still able to understand. Also, through translation, modern Western readers confront a strange and exciting literary reality. Both the East and the West can understand each other in her writing.

Her Islamic readers will be mostly women. For El Saadawi, men and women, while different, are fundamentally equal. An Arab man with that point of view is likely to be labeled a eunuch. One element of the terrorist mind I have not yet emphasized is the intense masculine fear of women. It drives many of their actions. The most frightening thing about the United States to the Islamic terrorist is the freedom of women. What if that should happen in Moslem countries? They would have to associate with women as equals—unthinkably frightening.

However, in the West, El Saadawi appeals to both men and women. In the war on terrorism she is an important ally, even though she does not support the war. She is a feminist with an Islamic voice. She can do more for women with her literary reality than any political or intellectual abstraction.

Doris Lessing had this to say about El Saadawi's novel, *The Fall of the Imam*: "This novel is unlike any other I have read, more like a poem or a lamenting ballad, with something hypnotic about it, with its rhythmic, keening language. This is a wonderful book and I hope a great many people will read it."

The Koran and a body of archaic poetry is the literary culture of most Arabs. It wasn't until the 1950s that novels were recognized in the Arab world. This is the moment for a literary renaissance to take place in Islam. And women readers will be the catalysts.

Many Arab writers have received Western language educations. They tend to write Western literature in the Arabic language. El Saadawi writes from the deepest stream of Arabian culture. She is a boundary-crosser and could become a Sharazad for world literature. She seeks a truth she can never find. She and each individual reader grow together. Remember, the Golden Age of Moslem literature in the 1100s was when the Jew, Maimonides, brought Arab, Jewish, and Christian writers together in Spain. Today El Saadawi could help inspire a new Golden Age, mustering both Arabic and modern literature to understand and learn from each other.

El Saadawi graduated from the University of Cairo as a medical doctor in 1955. Three years later she was appointed to the Ministry of Health and became the national Health Director. She left government service in 1972 because of her writings. In 1981 she was briefly imprisoned, also because of her writings. The following year, El Saadawi formed the Arab Woman's Solidarity Association. The government took it over in 1991.

Nawal El Saadawi has been awarded several national and international literary prizes, has lectured in many universities, and participated in many international and national conferences. Her works have been translated into many languages all over the world, and some of them are taught in a number of universities in different countries.

These universities include, in Egypt: The American University in Cairo, Cairo University, Ain Sham University in Cairo; in the United States: Duke University, The University of Washington in Seattle, Harvard University, Yale University, New York University, Columbia University, The University of California at Berkeley, The University of Illinois, Georgetown University, The University of Virginia, UCLA, Indiana University.

El Saadawi has written for the last fifty years. At age thirteen she wrote her first novel, *Memoirs of a Female Child Named Su ad*, which was later published. She has written short stories, novels, plays, memoirs, travelogues, and critical essays.

Nawal El Saadawi's words call upon the wonderful, inextinguishable, but still vulnerable glory of the human spirit, which goes beyond one culture to encompass both Islam and modernity. This spirit fills me with joy and hope. It is indeed the doom of the terrorist mind wherever it may exist. This is how Islam and modernity can work together—each enlarging and enriching the other.

Chapter 56

Stars Above

Literature is a way of sharing hearts. Nawal El Saadawi uses stars as symbols of hearts. She inspires me to do so as well, thinking of each individual heart as a star in the night sky.

Sultan is one from Damascus; he had the ability to include people from every religion and way of life without hatred, and is a star in mind's sky.

Monique, from Egypt, uses trust to confront the reality of hatred and contempt, and becomes a star.

Don, in the United States, was raised in a time and place of racial exclusion and fear. Through the use of yoga he has chosen diversity and charity toward all. He is a star.

In Israel, Shimon holds the hope for peace, a bright star.

Runi, from India, is a Hindu with many Moslem friends. Although they cannot think alike, they can trust each other.

Robert is from the Philippines. It was a fad to name Filipinos for American movie stars (Robert Montgomery.) He is a communist, but has chosen to fight Islamic terrorism. Like most Filipinos he is a potential friend of the United States. Hold out our hands to this star.

Leng is a Chinese Malaysian. Highly intelligent, she has chosen to trust modernity. It is her star.

Maryam is a star of trust to Iranian individuals. She has chosen literature to reach out.

Delores is a star of trust to all of her Islamic friends in Pakistan, Tunisia, and Algeria.

In Britain, Margaret works endlessly to bring literacy to young individuals, regardless of race and nationality.

Lansley, a Turkish graduate student, has become a star lighting the way to international trust.

Eceban, from Bosnia, seeks modernity for his country and has experimented with trust among individuals who can't think together.

Steve, teaching at Harvard, has taught his Islamic and modern students that they do not have to defend themselves in blocs, but can communicate through trust. He gets a star as does everyone on this list.

Elektra, in Macedonia, reveals to her seventh-grade students the way to give up hatred and trust Moslems.

A star to Bob, an American who is teaching in a school in Palestine. He has taught second-grade students to go beyond their hatreds by feeling angry each morning without being angry at anything or anybody.

Helenka, born in Germany, is working on getting individuals to include those beyond their national origins.

I'm sorry, but Saudi Arabia does not have any stars that I'm aware of. Surely there are some, perhaps in hiding.

At any rate, my sky is full of stars, stars beyond my knowing. They blind me with their brilliance and let me feel all the kindly individuals who can trust and come together in this war against terrorism. I hope you can feel this way too. It is a blessing.

In Memoriam
Sultan Succar

by Patton Howell

So let us go down
To the lake again.
It was a daily walk
Of his faith.

A reminder of the
Wide world he traveled,
"I climbed the Golan Heights,
In my youth."

But always with dignity
And grace, we suspect.
Always with a zest for life,
Was Sultan.

Here we are at the
Bench where he would sit.
For on this bench with Sultan,
Is room enough

For all the people of this earth.

Appendix 1

Some Arabic Books Available in English Translations

Shehadeh, Raja
> *From Occupation to Interim Accords: Israel and the Palestinians*
> *Samed: Journal of a West Bank Palestinian*
> *Occupation*
> *Third Way: A Journal of Life in the West Bank*
> *West Bank and the Rule of Law: A Study*
> *Strangers in the House: Coming of Age in Occupied Palestine*

El Saadawi, Nawal
> *The Circling Song*
> *Death of an Ex-Minister.* Translated by Shirley Eber
> *The Fall of the Imam.* Translated by Sherif Hetata
> *God Dies by the Nile.* Translated by Sherif Hetata
> *The Hidden Face of Eve: Women in the Arab World.*
> Translated by Sherif Hetata
> *The Innocence of the Devil.* Translated by Sherif Hetata
> *Memoirs of a Woman Doctor.* Translated by Catherine Cobham
> *Memoirs from the Women's Prison.* Translated by Marilyn Booth
> *My Travels Around the World.* Translated by Shirley Eber
> *Searching.* Translated by Shirley Eber
> *She Has No Place in Paradise.* Translated by Shirley Eber
> *Two Women in One.* Translated by Osman Nusairi and Jana Gough
> *The Well of Life and the Thread.* Translated by Sherif Hetata
> *Woman at Point Zero.* Translated by Sherif Hetata
> *Love in the Kingdom of Oil.* Translated by Sherif Hetata

Appendix 2

PEN Chapters in the United States

PEN Center USA
672 South Lafayette Park Place
Suite 42
Los Angeles, CA 90057

Colorado Chapter
2341 South Street
Boulder, CO 80302

New Mexico Chapter
2860 Plaza Verde
Santa Fe, NM 87505

Oakland Chapter
P. O. Box 70531
Station D
Oakland, CA 94612-0531

Orange County Chapter
322 Prospect Park N.
Tustin, CA 92680

Texas Chapter
4222 Willow Grove Road
Dallas, TX 75220

Appendix 3

International P.E.N. Centres Worldwide

HEADQUARTERS: International P.E.N.
9/10 Charterhouse Buildings, Goswell Road
London EC1M 7AT, U.K.

Islamic P.E.N. Centres

AMERICAN P.E.N. CENTRE
Centre website: www.pen.org
Centre email: pen@pen.org
Secretary Michael Roberts
American P.E.N. Centre
568 Broadway (4th floor)
New York, N.Y. 10012, U.S.A.

BOSNIAN P.E.N. CENTRE
Centre email: krugpen@bih.net.ba
Secretary: Ferida Durakovic
PEN Centre of Bosnia and Herzegovina
Vrazova 1
Sarajevo 71 000, Bosnia-Herzegovina

EGYPTIAN P.E.N. CENTRE
Secretary: Professor Fatma Moussa-Mahmoud
Egyptian P.E.N. Centre
P.O. Box 348
Orman-Giza, Egypt

INDONESIAN P.E.N. CENTRE
Secretary: Dr. Toeti Heraty Noerhadi
Indonesian P.E.N. Centre
Jalan Camara 6
Jakarta Pusat, Indonesia

IRANIAN WRITERS IN EXILE P.E.N. CENTRE
Cenre email: manuchehr. sabetian@virgin.net
Secretary: Manuchehr Sabetian
Vice-President, Iranian Writers in Exile P.E.N. Centre
c/o The Rationalist Press Association
47 Theobald's Road
London WC1X 8SP, U.K.

KAZAKHSTAN P.E.N. CENTRE
President: Abdhizhamil Nurpeisov
Kazakhstan P.E.N. Centre
Tulebayeva 156, Apart. 7
480091 Almaty, Kazakhstan

PALESTINIAN P.E.N. CENTRE
Centre email: ipen@palnet.com
President: Hanan Awwad
Palestinian P.E.N. Centre
Al Khaldi Street # 4
Wadi Al Juz, Jerusalem

TATAR P.E.N. CENTRE
Secretary: Mr. Akhat Mushinski
Tatar P.E.N. Centre
Dekabristov str. 110, kv. 41.
420080 Kazan, Tatarstan, C.I.S.

TURKISH P.E.N. CENTRE
Centre email: karantay@boun.edu.tr
Secretary: Suat Karantay
P.E.N. Yazarlar Dernegi
General Yazgan Sokak 10/10
Tunel 80050 Istanbul, Turkey

About the Author

Dr. Patton Howell graduated with a degree in international relations from Princeton University, studied at the Harvard Business School, and received his Ph.D. in psychology from Saybrook Institute. He became a staff correspondent for the United Press and later became an international consultant, and a nominator for the Nobel Prize Committee on Literature.

In 1989 he published *War's End*, a book predicting the fall of the Berlin Wall. It showed that changes in the way a critical number of people think can guide international affairs, rather than government policy guiding international affairs. Russia actually collapsed as he predicted, through spontaneous uprisings of individual people. The book became a regional best seller with a Bonze Medal from the International Publishers Association. Now Dr. Howell is back with a new book, *The Terrorist Mind in Islam and Iraq*.